Handbook of Lovebirds

Contents

HANDBOOK OF LOVEBIRDS

DISEASES OF PARROTS

Front and back endpapers, frontispiece: Peach-faced Lovebirds, photos by Dr. Herbert R. Axelrod.

ISBN 0-87666-820-1

© Horst Muller-Verlag, Bomlitz, Germany. Originally published in German under the title *Papageien und Grosssittich-Zucht—Unser Hobby, Band 1: Unzertrennliche—Agapornis / Krankheiten der Papgeienvogel.*
© 1982 T.F.H. Publications, Inc., Ltd. for the English translation. A considerable amount of new material has been added to this English-language edition, including but not limited to additional photographs. Copyright is also claimed for this new material.

Translated by Christa Ahrens

In the photo captions of this English-language edition, the nomenclature of the color varieties of the Peach-faced Lovebird follows the recommendations of the Terminology Committee of the African Lovebird Society. Inquiries about the activities of the Society should be addressed to Box 142, San Marcos, CA 92069.

Photographs (unless otherwise indicated): Dr. Herbert R. Axelrod, Horst Bielfeld, Siegfried Bischoff, Thomas Brosset, Wolfgang de Grahl, Kurt Hoppe, B. van de Kamer, Horst Muller. Disease section: Dr. med. vet. Manfred Heidenreich, Dr. med. vet. Norbert Kummerfeld, Archiv Klinik fur Geflugel TiHo Hannover.

Distributed in the U.S. by T.F.H. Publications, Inc., 211 West Sylvania Avenue, PO Box 427, Neptune, NJ 07753; in England by T.F.H. (Gt. Britain) Ltd., 13 Nutley Lane, Reigate, Surrey; in Canada to the pet trade by Rolf C. Hagen Ltd., 3225 Sartelon Street, Montreal 382, Quebec; in Canada to the book trade by H & L Pet Supplies, Inc., 27 Kingston Crescent, Kitchener, Ontario N28 2T6; in Southeast Asia by Y.W. Ong, 9 Lorong 36 Geylang, Singapore 14; in Australia and the South Pacific by Pet Imports Pty. Ltd., P.O. Box 149, Brookvale 2100, N.S.W. Australia; in South Africa by Valid Agencies, P.O. Box 51901, Randburg 2125 South Africa. Published by T.F.H. Publications, Inc., Ltd., the British Crown Colony of Hong Kong.

HANDBOOK OF LOVEBIRDS
HORST BIELFELD

DISEASES OF PARROTS
DR. MANFRED HEIDENREICH

Left to right, top row: Abyssinian cock; Black-cheeked;
American Pied Light Green Peach-faced; Normal Peach-faced.
Second row: Abyssinian hen; Gray-headed cock; Masked;
American Pied Light Green Peach-faced. Third row: Peach-
faced, red-pied variant; Yellow Masked; Nyasa; Blue Masked.
Bottom row: Dutch Blue Peach-faced; Red-faced; Dutch Blue
Ino Peach-faced; American Yellow Peach-faced.

Introduction

The German word *Unzertrennliche* ("Inseparables") is a very apt name for the birds of the genus *Agapornis,* commonly known as lovebirds to English-speaking aviculturists. It's apt because these birds are virtually unable to survive without each other's company. They generally live in pairs and need the close proximity of their mates. They stick together through thick and thin, nestle up to one another, scratch and groom each other, and exchange frequent "kisses." Lovebirds—"loving birds, birds in love"—should never be kept singly; they should always be kept in pairs.

Lovebirds are among the most popular members of the parrot family where cagebirds are concerned. There are several reasons for this. One considerable asset is the small size of these African birds. Depending on species, they do not grow to more than 13 to 17 cm. This means that for one pair we can manage with a cage of the dimensions 100 x 60 x 50 cm. In other words, no apartment is too small for them.

Another reason for their popularity is their bright, clear colors. The basic color of all species is green, ranging from a strong moss-green to delicate pastel shades and yellow. Almost all have a "flushed" face or at least a red bill. Many of these birds derive their popular names from the plumage of the face and head: Gray-headed Lovebird, Masked Lovebird, Black-cheeked Lovebird, Red-faced Lovebird, and Peach-faced Lovebird. In the Masked, Nyasa, Black-cheeked, and Fischer's Lovebirds a bare white eye-ring and the white cere make the colors of the head and beak seem even more intense.

A third—and very important—reason for the great popularity of lovebirds is that they are both hardy and undemanding. The majority of these birds can actually be left in outdoor aviaries during the winter in many temperate areas if they have access to a frost-free room. The bulk of their diet can consist of seeds. They are also very partial to green food and twigs, using the bark as nesting material.

Some lovebirds readily and successfully breed, but others show little inclination to do so. All of them should be provided with a nest box (of the same type as that used for Budgerigars) which is clipped over the cage or hung up inside the aviary. Courtship, nesting-material collection, and brood care are all very interesting to watch. In fact, with some lovebirds certain aspects of these behaviors are still unobserved or have so far remained unexplained.

To keep lovebirds, we must have the desire to study their peculiarities and their loving behavior towards one another. While growing very tame even as a pair, they never really become attached to their keeper in the way an individually kept Budgerigar would. Their "heart," after all, belongs to their mate, and it is the mate who receives all their attention. If we take the mate away, or from the outset try our luck with a single bird, we are left with only "half a bird"! The lone bird will never be able to develop its full charm and liveliness.

Lovebirds have little aptitude for and interest in learning to "talk." They do not develop any close contact with humans that would make them wish to "speak" with us. If a lovebird does learn to talk, it is usually from another parrot in whose company it is being kept. For want of a fellow lovebird, the love-hungry little creature takes this parrot into its heart and endeavors to learn its language.

The lovebirds belong to the genus *Agapornis,* which was established by Selby in 1836. Their scientific name—like their English name "lovebirds," their German name *Unzertrennliche,* and the names given to them in other languages—expresses how these birds caress each other (with what remarkable fervor!), how they nestle up to one another, and how they carry out all their activities together. In short, they behave like lovers.

In the order of parrots (Psittaciformes) the lovebirds belong to the family of pigmy parrots (Micropsittidae) in which, together with the genus *Loriculus* (hanging parrots), they form the subfamily of lovebirds. As pointed out by Dr. Hans E. Wolters in his work *Die Vogelarten der Erde* ("Birds of the World"), we still require further confirmation that the subfamilies woodpecker parrots (Micropsittinae), ground parrots (or tiger parrots, Psittacellinae), and lovebirds (Loriculinae) should in fact be classified together as a family. According to the present state of knowledge, these subfamilies do appear to be so closely related that it would seem justified to regard them as a single family.

Some hobbyists already familiar with lovebirds and their Latin names may be puzzled by the names of species, or rather their endings, as set down in this book: *swindernianus* instead of *swinderniana, pullarius* in place of *pullaria, canus* instead of *cana,* and *personatus* for *personata.* In Dr. Wolters' list of species the masculine endings *-us* have been used because ten years or so ago the Commission on International Zoological Nomenclature decided that generic names ending in *-is* (hence also *Agapornis*) should be treated strictly as masculine. Therefore the correct specific names are *swindernianus, pullarius, canus* and *personatus. Agapornis taranta* has retained its *-a* because *taranta* refers to its origin (*i.e.,* the name means "the one that comes from Taranta") and is not employed as, for example, in *Agapornis personatus,* "the masked one."

As in Dr. Wolters' book, so in this one too, the lovebirds are presented in a sequence that shows their relationship to each other. Because of its highly specialized feeding habits, the Black-collared Lovebird is most closely related to the hanging parrots, which also live on fruit. The Abyssinian, Red-faced, and Gray-headed Lovebirds do not possess eye-rings, but what does distinguish them is sexual dimorphism (that is, male and female birds differ in appearance). These species carry hardly any nesting material into the nest, and when they do they transport it under the feathers of the whole body. They build only a nesting pad, not a domed nest. The Peach-faced Lovebird forms a link between the more primitive species already mentioned and the more highly developed species. It does not possess an eye-ring, but neither do the sexes differ in their plumage. The nesting material is carried under the rump feathers. The nest may or may not have a cover. Usually, however, the birds do not build their own nest but move into a weaver's nest. The four species with the naked eye-rings can be considered more highly developed. In these species males and females are of the same coloration (*i.e.,* there is no sexual dimorphism). They build extensive, domed nests in tree cavities, under roofs, and in palm fronds, but they will also make use of weavers' nests.

Lovebirds in the Wild

I saw them flitting away, Fischer's Lovebirds! This was in northern Tanzania, on my visit to East Africa. Again and again I was able to observe them through the binoculars, close by our lodge. There may have been about eight to ten birds in all, which kept reappearing among a group of umbrella acacias. In these trees hung the football-sized nests of Rufous-tailed Weavers *(Histurgops ruficauda),* and these nests seemed to interest the Fischer's Lovebirds. It was at the beginning of the rainy season in April. Presumably these four or five pairs of Fischer's Lovebirds intended to breed in the thick-walled nests of the weavers. Many times I tried to creep up on them and take photographs with a 500 mm telephoto lens, but they discovered me too soon every time, then emitted loud, shrill warning cries and then flew off amidst high-pitched twittering. They flew away at lightning speed, yet I was able to make out the orange-colored head, the green body, and the blue under wing coverts and rump very clearly. The most conspicuous characteristic, however, was their penetrating voices. I would have liked to have had a tent of elephant grass or reeds built for me among the trees used for nesting, but this proved inadvisable since we heard the roaring of lions in the immediate area around the lodge. The grass had already grown so tall that recumbent lions were easily overlooked. Although the latter had absolutely no objections to tourists travelling in a Rover, they did not like pedestrians in their territory. Thus my experiences with lovebirds in their African home remained confined to spotting and observing them.

Most lovebirds are usually found in small groups similar to the one I have just described; this is true during the breeding season as well. They are sociable birds and like to live and breed in small, loose colonies. Around their nesting sites they are fairly quiet, secretive birds. Some other species of lovebirds, like Fischer's Lovebirds, prefer to breed in the empty nests of weavers, or even in occupied weavers' nests. They are strong and cheeky enough to chase off the rightful owners and save themselves the labor of having to build their own nest. Those that do build their own nests choose the hollows of trees (notably the baobab tree) or build them under the roofs of huts, in palm fronds, and in the nests of swifts.

The Red-faced Lovebird follows a different method altogether. With its bill it burrows deeply into an arboreal termitarium, making a passage with an attached chamber. The termites do not harm the birds. On the contrary, they ensure that the temperature inside the breeding chamber remains constant at 30° C.—a fact which should be noted by breeders of this species.

As already mentioned in discussing the relationship of the individual species, some lovebirds carry a lot of nesting material into their nests and others hardly any at all. Some transport the material in their bills, while others carry it in the feathers of the rump or in the small feathers all over the body.

The eggs—usually white in color, roundish, and numbering four to six—are incubated solely by the hen. The chicks remain in the nest for about forty to fifty days and are then fed by the parents for about another two weeks.

Grass seeds, millet, corn, rice, and cereal crops form the diet of lovebirds in the wild, as do acacia seeds, berries, and diverse fruits. Nearly all the lovebirds regard figs and/or their seeds as particularly desirable, and for the Black-collared Lovebird this food is essential to survival. Apart from these foods, the birds also appreciate tender shoots, leaf buds, and petals. Many lovebirds enjoy insects and their larvae, especially when there are chicks to feed.

In cereal, millet, corn, and rice fields lovebirds may gather in flocks of 100 to 200 birds and become serious pests. Far worse than the damage they cause through eating is the incidental destruction of crops. Because of their intelligence, alertness, and speed they usually manage to escape unhurt when the farmers go after them.

While some species inhabit the dry steppes and savannahs and fly to the watering places morning and night, others live in the immediate vicinity of water, i.e., in the trees along the shore. Lovebirds are creatures of habit, and once they have chosen a cavity or a nest they roost there as long as they can.

The majority of lovebirds are regarded as nonthreatened species in their natural habitats. They are, however, more common in some areas than in others. The smallest range is that of the four species with white eye-rings. They are in need of protection, particularly the Black-cheeked Lovebird which is the most endangered. Like most lovebirds, it should no longer be taken from the wild but should be propagated by fanciers. One day, perhaps, it will then be possible to release rare lovebirds in their native ranges and thus help prevent their extinction.

A pair of Peach-faced Lovebirds.

Umbrella acacias in the Serengeti,
nesting trees of Fischer's Lovebirds.

Keeping Lovebirds

Lovebirds are pretty little parrots which tempt many bird fanciers into buying a pair so that they can enjoy their colors and their endearing and lively behavior. If the lovebirds will be kept indoors, remember that some species have very loud and shrill voices. Often this screeching is uttered with such perseverance that the hobby embarked upon with such expectation is hastily abandoned. On the other hand, anyone setting up an aviary in the garden should think of the neighbors. There are sure to be complaints if the aviary stands too close to a neighbor's yard and there has been no prior consultation regarding the possible noise.

Plenty of room should be available to the lovebirds. In this respect, too, many mistakes are made by the optimistic new hobbyist, as indeed by the dealer as well. As discussed in detail below, one gets what one deserves if these parrots are squeezed into cages of inadequate size. The birds are not ornaments but living creatures which by nature fly about a great deal—in other words, they need exercise.

Because of the frequently quarrelsome disposition of these birds, anyone who intends to keep—and perhaps even breed—several pairs or a small flock of lovebirds needs to have a sufficient number of empty accommodations in reserve. All keepers and breeders of these birds complain about lack of space.

People who love these birds also have to put up with their disadvantages, but there are plenty of attractive and interesting aspects that make keeping them worthwhile.

CAGES AND AVIARIES

Lovebirds can be kept in cages as well as in an aviary. The cage must not be too small. Some authors have described cages which measure 70 x 50 x 40 cm as sufficient even for rearing chicks. While these chicks may have survived, the birds certainly did not have enough room for the exercise and other forms of self-expression that are vital to them and for

which we love them. Lovebirds kept in cages which are cramped and unsuitable very soon lose most of their characteristically varied, lively behavior. They grow dull and eventually do nothing but hop to and fro in a habitual manner. These birds are particularly likely to become mutual pluckers, self-pluckers, screechers, and even self-mutilators or cannibals. It is hard to believe that people can thoughtlessly squeeze the birds (which, after all, they bought out of interest and for their enjoyment) into cages that are much too small and then wonder why the birds do not come up to expectations. Much of the blame must go to those who are responsible for manufacturing cages that are too constricted and generally unsuitable. Most of them still seem to be perpetuating the mistakes their grandfathers made.

Cages intended for lovebirds should be at least 100 cm long, 60 cm high, and 50 cm wide. These dimensions would allow a pair to move freely about and even to use their wings a little. Better still would be a cage which measures 120 x 90 x 60 cm, especially if it is to be a permanent residence and possible breeding place.

There are two types of cages which, in very different ways, are particularly suitable for lovebirds. The first is the metal wire cage most commonly available in pet shops. The cage must be the correct size and have a plastic base that is sufficiently high to not allow the birds to scatter seed husks and small feathers with every move. It must also have horizontal wire bars; these enable the birds to use all the walls for climbing and thus increase their opportunities for exercise.

Another advantage of the metal wire cage is that it does not require its own lighting. It is sufficient to place it in a bright spot and the birds will get enough light—even unfiltered sunlight if the cage is located by an open window, on a balcony, or on a terrace. One disadvantage of the wire cage is that the birds are easily exposed to drafts; another is that they do not feel secure inside it. These two drawbacks, however, depend of course on the cage's location.

The alternative is the box cage: a cupboard-like container with a front of metal bars, glass, or transparent plastic. This type of cage can easily be made by the hobbyist himself, the basic requirement being a cupboard that is no longer needed for its original purpose. It is advisable to equip the lower portion of the front with sliding doors (of glass or transparent plastic). Then sand, husks, nesting material, and small feathers do not drop on the floor and make the room look unsightly. A drawer on the bottom, made of hard plastic and with a high edge, serves the same purpose. A sheet metal drawer or a drawer made of plastic-covered wood is on the whole too heavy. Alternatively—and this is a better solution than the use of a drawer—the cage floor can be covered with a plastic tile. Then there is no danger of any dampness getting into the (usually) wooden floor. Cleaning a cage without a bottom drawer is no problem nowadays; it is easy enough to remove the sand and dirt with a vacuum cleaner. Anyone who owns several cages and indoor flights will appreciate one of those powerful vacuum cleaners where the waste material is sucked straight into a large tank.

Above the sliding glass doors of the box cage there should be doors spanned with wire mesh. Doors that swing open are best. Alternatively, one can use removable gates. These are simple to fit and can be taken out when the cage is cleaned or the perches or twigs removed.

One very important feature of any cage is that it should be able to be subdivided by a sliding partition through the center, made either of wood or hard plastic. Wire mesh may also be used. A firm partition comes in handy for inspecting the nest, cleaning the cage, or catching one of the birds. It ensures that the birds in the other half of the cage do not become unduly alarmed. When two birds need to get used to each other, or when almost-independent young birds still being fed are already being chased and bitten, a sliding partition of not too small a mesh can prove very helpful.

A box cage should be fitted with a source of light; otherwise, the cage may be too dark for the birds to live in. Depending on the size of the cage, fluorescent tubes of 15 to 20 watts are suitable. A practical, compact fixture can be attached to the ceiling toward the front of the cage.

Any room that is dry, free from drafts, and reasonably bright is suitable for conversion into an indoor aviary. How big the individual quarters are and how they are divided up depends largely on the sort of accommodation that is available. What is important, however, is that they be readily accessible and easy to clean. Lovebirds do not need excessive amounts of space. A pair having an area of 100 x 150 cm and room height stands the best chance of breeding successfully. If several pairs are to be housed in flights that are adjacent to each other, it is advisable to use wooden or non-transparent polyester panels rather than wire mesh for the partitions. During the breeding season the birds constantly hang on the wire and try to bite each other. There is also a danger of foot injuries if there is nothing but a single wire mesh between the compartments. If wire mesh is to be used, then a double layer should be fitted, with a space of about 8 cm between the two layers.

While lovebirds do not have the same habit of gnawing wood as Budgerigars, it is still a good idea to use hardwood for all projecting wooden structures including door frames. Alternatively, the latter may be protected with L-shaped aluminum strips. Some lovebird breeders have used steel angle-irons or tubing for the framing of their aviaries.

Although indoor aviaries generally have floors of firm material, this is often not the case where garden aviaries are concerned. The floors of outdoor aviaries tend to consist of garden soil which is sometimes covered with a layer of sand or overgrown with grass. This has distinct advantages for the birds and can be very good for their health. It can, however, be dangerous too. For one thing, the ground can gradually become saturated with droppings and grow contaminated as a result. (Wild birds perching on the aviary may also cause contamination.) Then there is the vermin problem; mice, rats, weasels, and other

Lovebirds frequently breed in the
nests of Rufous-tailed Weavers.

Hollows in old monkey-bread trees
are favored by many lovebirds.

animals are able to get inside the aviary. While some merely come to take food, others prey on the birds as well. It is wiser, therefore, to have a concrete floor and to build a solid foundation for the framework of the aviaries.

Garden aviaries for lovebirds should have a height of about 2 m and measure 150 x 100 cm in length and width if they are to house one pair of breeding birds. For larger numbers of the same species an aviary can never be big enough. The more flying space the birds have the more natural their behavior will be and the less likely are they to fight with each other.

What has been said about indoor aviaries also holds true for outdoor ones: if several adjacent flights are to be occupied, it is essential to separate them either by means of a solid partition or with a double layer of wire mesh. The two layers of mesh should be at least 6 cm apart. Otherwise, as already pointed out earlier, the birds may sustain foot injuries.

For garden aviaries a construction of solid steel angle-iron or steel tubing is, of course, more durable than anything else. However, specially treated wooden beams may also be used. To prevent the birds from damaging the wood through chewing, wire mesh should be nailed on from the inside. As an alternative one can use the L-shaped aluminum strips already mentioned.

Part of the outdoor aviary should be covered with translucent polyester sheets to protect the birds from rain. The sides exposed to the weather (north and west) should be closed, particularly where the birds do not have an indoor aviary or a shelter at their disposal. In most cases it is possible to build the aviaries onto a house, wall, or garage on these sides. Then little additional work or material is required to protect the birds from rain, storms, hail, and snow. A closed corner also affords a certain amount of protection against the cold. Materials that can be used for this purpose (some of which have already been mentioned) are translucent polyester sheets, wood, and reed-matting.

Garden flights that are connected to indoor aviaries are ideal. The birds can be indoors or outdoors, just as they wish. In really cold weather the birds may be kept entirely inside, which is necessary for certain species and will do no harm in the case of the hardier ones either.

ESSENTIAL AND USEFUL ACCESSORIES

Both cages and aviaries should be equipped with suitable perches. Hardwood dowels may be used. They are not chewed quite so quickly by the lovebirds and are easy to clean. The dowels should vary in thickness; a diameter of 14 mm would form the right average. Since lovebirds greatly enjoy chewing (and, ultimately, destroying) twigs, fresh branches and twigs from various broad-leaved trees are always welcome as perches. While gathering them creates a little extra work for the fancier, it is well worth the effort. These natural perches have so much to offer to the birds: a lot more to occupy themselves with, excellent food, nesting material, and invaluable exercise (since the birds are obliged to adopt a variety of holds and positions on the ramified branches). Twigs and branches of willow, poplar, linden, mountain-ash, fruit trees, and many other broad-leaved trees are suitable. Since the bark will be chewed off and eaten, the branches should be washed and dried thoroughly before use. In spacious indoor and outdoor aviaries big, ramified branches may be put into buckets with water and stones; the buckets are placed on the floor or into Christmas-tree or sun-shade stands. The branches may be fixed to the walls with fittings of hardwood, plastic, or metal such as are used for thick curtain rods, on which the curtains are hung by thick rings. I have been using these for some time and never cease to be amazed at how easy and quick it is to change the branches. A single screw is loosened, the old branch is pulled out, a new one inserted, and that is all there is to it.

The floors of cages and aviaries should be covered with fine sand. In garden aviaries many breeders leave the natural soil as it is. There is no objection to this, provided the aviary is rat- and mouse-proof (*i.e.,* if it has a deep foundation, or a buried skirt of tarred wire-netting surrounds it). Also, the top layer of the soil should be replaced one spade-cut deep once or twice a year (depending on

Lovebirds find ideal nest sites
in these old acacias.

population size). Some breeders like to cover the floors of their aviaries with fir or larch needles. In the majority of cases the floors of garden aviaries will consist partially of sand (especially under the perches) and partially of turf or earth.

Food and water containers should be made of glazed clay or porcelain. Oval porcelain dishes 10 cm long or the larger glazed flowerpot saucers are most suitable. Those measuring about 20 cm in diameter are also very useful as baths and drinking vessels. For germinated and soft food only very shallow dishes should be used; otherwise these foods quickly turn sour. I use the glass lids of canning jars for them.

All bowls for lovebirds should be made of clay, porcelain, or glass. Anything lighter, such as sheet metal or plastic, is readily and "deliberately" upset by the birds.

What has been said about bowls also applies to automatic feeding devices. They must be heavy and consist of a material (hard plastic or metal) that withstands the strong bills of the lovebirds. If they are made of the right material, seed hoppers are convenient for hobbyists who do not have the time and opportunity to feed their birds every day. If a cage houses a pair of birds, the common plastic feeding tubes can simply be hooked over the wire from the outside to dispense both food and water. Then only the small, firm feeding-end juts into the cage.

Box cages and indoor aviaries will almost always require some form of illumination. Light is an important factor not only for triggering the breeding mood and ensuring success but also for the general well-being of the birds. Every box cage with a length of about 100 cm and a height of 60 to 80 cm should be fitted with a 15-watt fluorescent tube. For larger cages 20 watts will be required. The lamp should be located under the ceiling toward the front of the cage. For aviaries, fluorescent tubes of 40 to 65 watts are most suitable (the exact wattage depends on aviary size). These tubes measure 120 or 150 cm in length. An ideal amount of light would be 20 watts per square meter at an aviary height of 2 to 2.5 m.

The best sources of light for birds are the wide-spectrum tubes from America that became available a few years ago. For their wattage they give a very bright light. Above all, however, the light they emit largely approximates sunlight. This means they also supply the birds with a certain amount of ultraviolet rays which are essential for good feather growth and absolutely vital for the body's own production of the necessary vitamin D. These tubes are available from pet shops.

Another very important device for the breeder is a timer which automatically turns the light on or off in cages and aviaries in the morning and at night. If this timer is equipped with two circuits, it can also be used to provide a night light. This, which can be very dim, makes it possible for the birds to become orientated at all times. There will be no panic-stricken flying-about, such as often occurs in complete darkness for the slightest reason (unfamiliar noises or movements). For night lights I use 10-watt bulbs like those found in refrigerators and ovens; these have always given excellent results.

The timer is not only for the convenience of the bird keeper but also is of considerable importance to the birds. In their tropical home lovebirds get almost exactly twelve hours of sunlight and twelve hours of darkness per day. For those species that live farthest from the equator, this varies by (at most) two hours, depending on the time of year. Lovebirds kept in indoor aviaries should, therefore, not be exposed to more than twelve to fourteen hours of daylight either. They need uninterrupted ten- to twelve-hour periods of sleep if they are to remain lively and in good health.

GENERAL CARE

Anyone who acquires birds—that is, more than just one or two in a small cage—has chosen a very nice, interesting, and rewarding hobby. However, there are two sides to every coin and that applies to birdkeeping too. As a birdkeeper, you will be required to put yourself out rather more than you may be prepared to do. Birds are living creatures that need attention, food, and care every single day. Unlike, for example, a stamp collection, they cannot be left inside a drawer for a short or long period. A great deal of your spare time will have to be devoted to looking after the birds, for no aspect of their care can ever be allowed to be postponed or forgotten.

When a large number of lovebirds is kept, you cannot take the birds to friends or relatives to be looked after when you go on vacation. Obviously these birds inhabit large cages, probably even aviaries in the house or in a garden. You will, therefore, need to find someone to take your place while you are away—someone who knows how to look after lovebirds. If this is not possible, you will just have to go without your vacation.

The beauty of keeping lovebirds is the constant opportunity it affords to observe their way of life and behavior. However, their daily care should give pleasure too; this includes seeing how the birds thrive and, maybe, reproduce themselves.

Caring for these birds involves such daily tasks as providing them with food and water, removing remnants of perishable food and wilted old greens. During the breeding season fresh nesting material must be supplied every day; the majority of lovebirds need this in order to keep the humidity inside the nest box at a certain level. In addition, the thermometer, hygrometer, and lights and timers should be checked daily. Keep the birds under close observation. Where applicable, also have a look inside the nest boxes every day.

Once a week all the perches should be washed or changed. Replace the sand in all cages. Rake through the sand, soil, or grass in the aviaries.

Once a month the birds' accommodations should be disinfected. The turf sods covering the concrete in indoor and outdoor aviaries should be replaced, likewise the sand in indoor and outdoor aviaries.

Old nesting sites should be inspected at three-month intervals. Old, dirty nests must be cleaned and disinfected. Also every three months, the wire mesh and aviary construction must be checked for weaknesses and holes since most lovebirds have strong bills and chew constantly.

Twice a year the soil in garden aviaries with natural ground should be removed one spade deep and replaced with fresh soil. Wood and metal should be painted to prevent rotting or rusting. If you plan certain tasks for certain days of the week or month, the danger of forgetting or postponing them is not so great. You are advised to draw up a timetable for yourself and adhere to it strictly. Birds—notably parrots which, of course, includes the lovebirds—become adapted to the routine which you practice. They then accept the necessary disturbances much more calmly than they would if you were to descend upon them out of the blue at unaccustomed times. The same holds true for feeding. This, too, should be carried out at the same time each day.

Incubating birds can be very shy and sensitive to the slightest disturbance. When this is the case you should not do anything around them; merely hand them their food and drink. Otherwise breeding may not be successful.

CORRECT NUTRITION

Seeds: The basic food for all lovebirds is a mixture of dried seeds which consists of canary seed, various kinds of millet (white, yellow, red, Senegal, and Japanese), hulled oats, and a few sunflower and hemp seeds. It is important to make sure that this basic food is always available in adequate amounts. Lovebirds like to have a good selection of seeds. For this reason the seeds can also be offered to them separately or mixed in bowls or hoppers. There is no danger of the birds eating too much of this basic food and getting fat as a result.

Lovebirds are particularly fond of millet sprays. These are accepted with great enthusiasm especially when there are young in the nest box or the young have just left the nest.

Grass seeds, which form part of the lovebirds' staple diet in their natural habitat, are not usually found fully matured but occur

Lovebirds enjoy building large domed nests
in the midst of a whorl of palm fronds.

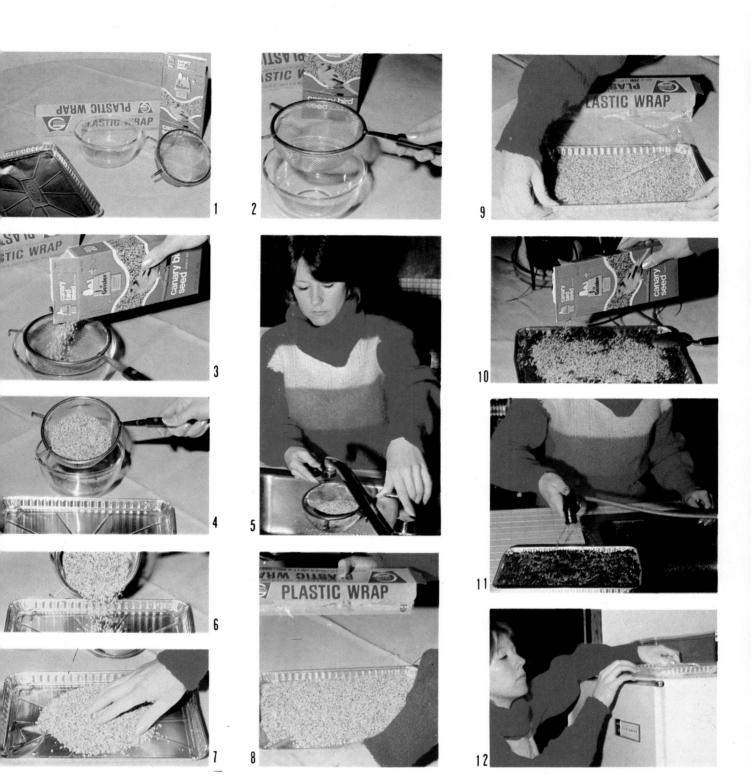

Seed Germination requires any birdseed which is fresh. You also require (1) an aluminum tray, a strainer, bowl, and plastic wrap. The strainer must fit into the bowl and be able to support itself (2) on the rim. Fill the strainer with the birdseed (3,4), and rinse it under running water until it is thoroughly clean (5). Allow it to soak for about a day in the bowl. Change the water as frequently as convenient, but at least once every 12 hours. Then pour the dampened seed onto the tray (6) and spread the seed uniformly (7). Mix in any mold-inhibiting substance (Moldex) and cover the seed to keep the moisture in, but not to stop air from getting to the seed (8,9). If you want to grow *grass* from the seed you can use earth; sprinkle it with seed (10), mix the seed with the earth, sprinkle lightly with water (11) and store in a warm, dark place (12). The seed used with earth can either be soaked for a while (see above 1 through 5), or straight from the box.

in all stages of development from milky to hard. Only when droughts make the savannahs dry up are the lovebirds dependent on the hard seeds that lie on the ground. So that we can offer them a substitute for the tastier and more easily digested immature seeds, we should prepare germinated seeds for them.

Germinated seeds: The preparation of germinated seeds is incredibly simple. Depending on the size of the bird population, three to four plastic sieves (which are available in different sizes) and plastic bowls to match are required. Into the first sieve we put the quantity of dry mixed seeds normally eaten in one day. The sieve is placed inside the bowl and sufficient water poured over to cover all the seeds. If these preparations are started in the morning, the seeds should be rinsed thoroughly with cold water at night and the following morning. After having been allowed to expand in the water for twenty-four hours, the seeds are drained and again left to stand. To prevent the seeds from drying out, the sieve is covered with a piece of glass or plastic. Thorough rinsing should be continued at twelve-hour intervals. Depending on the room temperature, the germinated seeds will be ready for use after two or three days from the start of their preparation. After the final rinse the sieve containing the germinated seeds is placed on a bath towel which has been folded several times to allow most of the moisture to drain off.

To ensure a daily supply of germinated seeds, two to three sieves will be constantly in use. From time to time the bowls and sieves should be cleaned thoroughly with a brush and hot water to which some disinfectant has been added. If all utensils are clean and the seeds are rinsed at regular intervals, the germinated seeds should always remain fresh. Prior to being germinated, seeds have a slightly sweetish, nutty odor. Germinated seeds that have gone off, on the other hand, smell rotten. With most other methods the wet seeds frequently turn sour and decompose. This kind of food is at its most valuable when the sprouts have just broken through the kernels. The germinating process results in the formation of vitamins, and the seeds open up so that the starch they contain becomes easier to digest. Germinated

seeds are, therefore, nutritionally preferable to dry seeds. They are particularly valuable as a rearing food for young birds.

Green Food and Food Plants: Green food, fruit, berries, leaf buds, and the juicy bark of various broad-leaved trees are all popular foods with lovebirds. The green food they like comprises chickweed, young dandelion leaves, lettuce, endive, spinach, and many other plants. All green food must be washed thoroughly before it is given to the birds. There is always a danger that it may have been treated with chemicals which are often toxic to birds.

Particular favorites of lovebirds are various grasses when their panicles contain seeds which are either half-ripe or newly ripened. Along with grasses, the birds also enjoy other wild plants with seeds in different stages of maturation. These include chickweed, cress, sorrel, greater plantain, ribwort plantain, shepherd's purse, sow thistle, orache, and mugwort. Some of these weeds can always be found between spring and late autumn; they are all very nutritious and add variety to the birds' fare. Many birds literally pounce on the seed-bearing parts of these plants.

Anyone who owns a garden with a sheltered south side can grow various kinds of millet, canary seed, and perhaps even sunflowers and harvest his own ripe or nearly ripe seed sprays. It goes without saying that the plants with the ripening seeds must be protected from sparrows, but this can readily be accomplished with the aid of nylon netting. When the sprays, panicles, and sunflowers have been collected, they can either be given to the birds straightaway or stored in a freezer for use in the breeding season or during the winter months when they serve to enrich the birds' diet with vitamins.

Regarding fruit, almost all kinds are eaten by lovebirds. Apples, pears, bananas, oranges, mandarins, grapes, plums, peaches, cherries, and strawberries are special favorites. Dried fruit is also liked, most especially figs (they love not only the flesh but also the seeds). Dates and sultanas are accepted too. Lovebirds like nothing better than ripe mountain-ash berries, rosehips, elderberries,

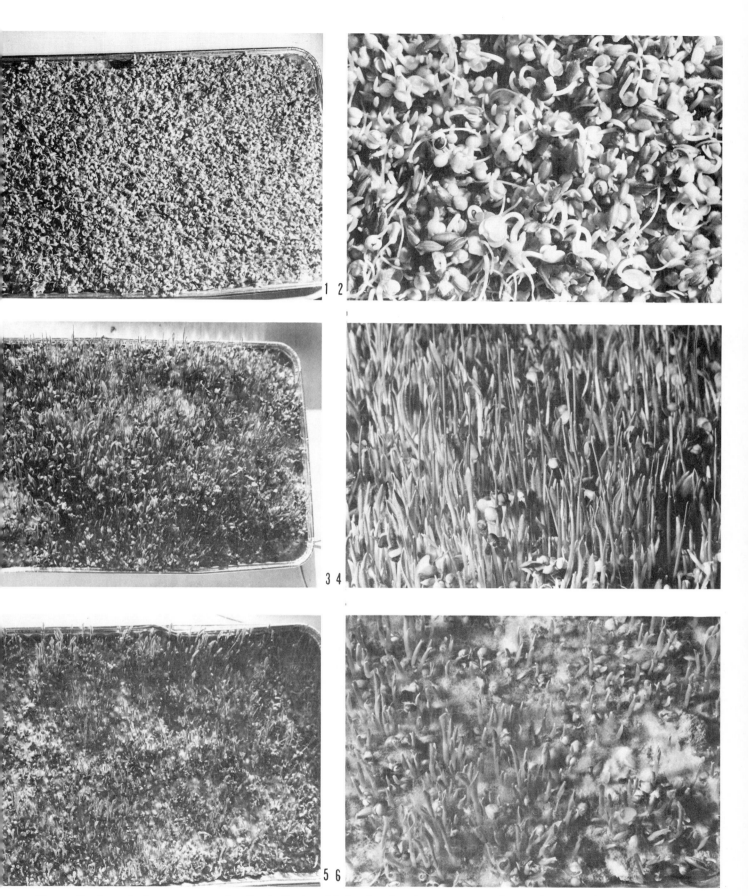

Green foods and plants are popular foods for lovebirds. An aluminum tray can be used to germinate seeds as per the method shown on page 21. Photo 1 above shows the tray with the seeds germinated; photo 2 is a closeup of the actual seeds. This is the best food available for lovebirds. Photos 3 and 4 show the tray with seeds planted in a little soil. This grows into a grass which is very acceptable to lovebirds. Photos 5 and 6 show a tray which has become moldy and unsuitable for feeding.

Lovebirds use many of the same products
(grit, or gravel, in this case) as are
marketed for Budgerigars (parakeets).

Gnawing on a mineral block not only helps keep
the bird's beak in shape but also supplies
necessary minerals and trace elements.

Cuttlebone is one of the best sources of
calcium, which is important in feather
growth and formation of egg shells.

as well as hawthorne fruits. Amon
vegetables, the birds like carrots an
cucumbers as well as the leaves of Brusse
sprouts.

The twigs of willow, poplar, mapl
sycamore, mountain ash, hawthorr
blackthorne, oak, beech, linden, and, abov
all, fruit trees are chewed with enthusiasn
The bark of these trees is rich in minerals an
trace elements. If branches are put into wate
in winter or early spring, buds will soon ap
pear. The birds should be given this high
vitamin food at this time, and later too, whe
the trees outside come into bud.

Insectile food: Many lovebirds readily ac
cept insectile food. The larvae (mealworm
and pupae of the beetle *Tenebrio*, as well a
ant pupae, may be offered to birds that ar
rearing young. Ideally, however, a good com
mercial rearing food should be administerec
mixed with some grated carrot. A small por
tion of hard-boiled egg yolk and an insec
based soft food may also be added.

Vitamins: If the lovebirds receive adequat
amounts of green food, fresh twigs, ger
minated seeds, and seed-bearing grasses as we
as weeds, they will not require addition
vitamins. On the other hand, during th
breeding season or while molting or when th
birds are subjected to great fluctuations i
temperature and weather, it can do no harm t
mix a multivitamin preparation or vitamins c
the B-complex into their drinking water. On
to three drops per pair is an adequate dail
dose. It is better to administer vitamins i
small doses every day than in larger quantitie
once or twice a week.

Minerals and Trace Elements: The bird
should at all times have access to grit, th
crushed shells of boiled eggs, cuttlebone,
calcium block, well-rinsed old mortar, an
charcoal. Without these vital substances a bir
will not feel healthy, its digestion will b
disturbed, and the molt will cause great prot
lems if the bird survives it at all.

BATHING AND DRINKING WATER

Lovebirds drink quite a lot. They should always have fresh water at their disposal. Depending on the number of birds, the drinking water may be offered in automatic water dispensers (tube drinkers) of varying sizes. For larger populations in one aviary, water dispensers with a capacity of one liter or more are suitable.

Lovebirds make frequent use of their bathing facilities. Standard bird baths may be clipped onto the cage. Some lovebirds, however, dislike bathing in these; they prefer large, shallow dishes. Make sure that the bottom of these dishes is not too slippery. In other words, do not use a glazed porcelain or earthnware dish; instead provide a dish which has a rough bottom that gives the birds a foothold when they take their bath.

In warm weather it may be necessary to change the water in the bathing dish several times a day, as the birds drag a lot of dirt into the dish. It has proved advantageous to put a few big stones or some coarse gravel around the bathing vessel. Then the water stays clean for a longer period of time.

A lovebird cage should be large enough for its occupants and suited to the place in your home where you intend to keep it.

Because of their propensity for climbing, lovebirds prefer cages on which the wires run horizontally.

Many useful birdkeeping accessories are stocked by pet shops, ranging from necessities like food dishes to treats and toys for pet birds.

Breeding Lovebirds

If you wish to breed lovebirds, your most important requirement is to own a true pair. With species like the Abyssinian, Gray-headed and Red-faced Lovebirds this is no problem since the sexes are readily distinguished. When it comes to the four species with white eye-rings and the Peach-faced Lovebird, however, matters are rather different. These are the species most commonly kept and cultivated. If you are new to aviculture, none of the differentiating characteristics listed here are likely to help you. Nor is it very probable that you will be able to feel the greater or lesser width of the pelvis. The interactive behavior of two birds kept alone together also gives you no clue; two cocks or two hens can behave like a pair, often even feeding one another and copulating. The best advice one can give is that you buy a pair from an experienced breeder or ask an experienced breeder to help you with the purchase of a pair.

The birds should be at least nine to ten months old before being used for breeding or before being provided with a nest box. Females that are too young or that mate in garden aviaries when the temperatures are still on the low side tend to suffer from egg binding. Be patient and do not hang a nest box inside a young female's aviary too early. The same note of caution applies to young females that are to be bred at room temperature in indoor aviaries or cages.

Cages and aviaries used for breeding birds must be equipped as sensibly as possible so that the birds are not subjected to unnecessary disturbance. Make sure that the daily tasks such as feeding and the provision of water and nesting material are carried out quickly and efficiently. Changing the sand and cleaning the cage and aviary should not cause the birds to panic either. If everything has been conveniently designed and set up, there should be no problems.

When a single pair is to be bred in a cage it is best to attach the nest box to the outside. Otherwise, if the cage has a base of about 15 x 20 or 15 x 15 cm and a height of 20 or 25 cm, the nest box would take up too much room inside the cage. Fitting the nest box externally—and being able to pull down its back wall—also has the advantage of making nest inspection very easy.

An important prerequisite for breeding lovebirds inside a house or apartment is a high atmospheric humidity of between 60 and 70%. This is often difficult to achieve. Daily spraying of the nest box (which should have thick walls if possible) and then letting the moisture work in is a good method. The female herself helps to increase the dampness inside the nest box by bathing frequently and returning to the eggs with wet plumage. Daily supplies of fresh willow twigs or other nesting materials are chopped into small pieces by the female and carried into the nest box as required.

When the birds are bred in a garden aviary which is connected to an indoor aviary, the nest boxes may be located outside. If they hang on a shady side, they are exposed to relatively high atmospheric humidity. They also get the benefit of rain, and their thick walls can store a certain amount of moisture. During prolonged dry periods the nest boxes should be sprayed with water. Equally important is a constant supply of fresh nesting material.

If the indoor aviaries are in a building of solid stone, with a well-insulated roof, the nest boxes can be hung up inside them. In a wooden house the humidity can be so low in the summer that the chances of successful breeding are virtually nil. In such situations daily spraying of nest boxes or even the whole aviary is not sufficient. Indeed, it would merely lead to unacceptable fluctuations in atmospheric humidity. Far better in these circumstances would be an electric humidifier, although it has its limitations too: it raises the humidity a mere 10 to 20%. The best solution, undoubtedly, would be to use a special nest box that has a bottom of perforated galvanized sheet-metal and underneath it a water container made of galvanized sheet-metal or plastic. By means of the evaporating water the humidity inside the nest box is kept so high that hatching is guaranteed.

Finally, you are advised to select a spot from which you can observe the birds very clearly without being seen by them. It need hardly be pointed out that in the presence of human beings—even their familiar keeper—the birds behave differently than when they feel unwatched. What you need to see, however, is their natural behavior. It is this that allows you to draw conclusions as to how well matched a pair might be and how likely they are to breed successfully. The more you remain in the background, unseen by the birds and never disturbing them, the better are the breeding chances.

COURTSHIP, NEST BUILDING, EGG LAYING, AND INCUBATION

The courtship behavior of lovebirds, although showing minor variations from one species to another, is fairly uniform on the whole. At the beginning of the breeding season—and this applies to all species—the cocks start to feed the hens. Alternatively, a hen ready to breed may beg the cock to feed her (this, too, often happens). The pair rub against each other even more than usual. The cock is forever attending to the hen and before long does not leave her side at all.

Prior to actually mating, the birds patter to and fro on the perch, or on a horizontal branch, with increasing excitement. The cock flies alongside the hen every so often, describing a short curve and landing first on her left and then on her right side. He "sings" constantly—that is, he emits calls—and scratches his head. To scratch himself, he draws his foot behind and around the wing and thence to his head. This looks a little complicated but presents no problem to the bird at all.

The hen invites the cock to copulate with her by crouching on the branch, holding her tail erect, and bending her head back. She opens her wings to a greater or lesser degree and raises them slightly. Then the cock gets on the hen's back and holds onto her feathers with his toes and claws. The act of copulation is not over with in seconds, as in the case of finches, but lasts for at least one to two or in many cases even five minutes. The mating birds must on no account be disturbed; if the sex act is interrupted prematurely, fertilization does not take place.

With the exception of the Red-faced, all lovebirds go about nest building in a more or less identical fashion. In all species it is nearly always the hen who builds the nest. While the Red-faced is offered a piece of peat or a block of peat fibers held together with lime so that she can excavate a chamber, the other lovebirds are provided with nesting material which they can carry into the nest box. Such material will consist mostly of willow twigs, but twigs from other broad-leaved trees such as birches, poplars, mountain ashes, lindens, and fruit trees can be used equally well. Long, narrow strips of bark are chewed off these by the hens and transported either in the bill or under the feathers, depending on the species, into the nest box. Besides strips of bark, the birds also use leaves and leaf-strips, grasses and other wild plants (such as chickweed), as well as the needles of firs and pines. Even empty millet sprays and stalks, strips of paper, bits of straw, and, sometimes, coconut fibers are collected. The four species with white eye-rings carry the nesting material to the nest in their bills. The Peach-faced transports the nesting material under its rump feathers; this action, to a certain extent, has also been observed among Gray-headed and Abyssinian Lovebirds. The two latter species together with the Red-faced, however, vary in their enthusiasm when it comes to nest building and carry the nesting material in diverse places under the small body feathers or, sometimes, in the bill. The Red-faced, Gray-headed, and Abyssinian sometimes do not collect any nesting material at all or only enough to provide a pad for the

Masked Lovebird hen incubating.

A clutch of Fischer's Lovebird eggs.

Young Peach-faced Lovebirds, Normal
and Yellow, about eighteen days old.

Young Red-faced Lovebirds, about thirty
days old, in the nest and in the hand.

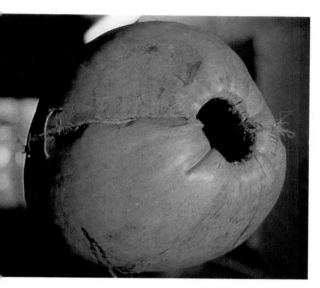

Coconut shells for nest building
are popular with lovebirds.

Rectangular nest boxes are practical
and liked by lovebirds. The floor
area should be at least 15 x 20 cm.

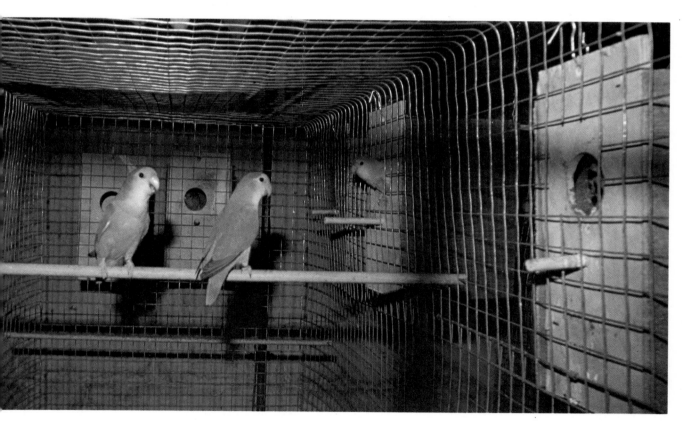

Nest boxes attached to the outside of this flight
housing a colony of breeding Peach-faced Lovebirds
(Dutch Blue) allow for easy nest inspection.

eggs. By contrast, the other species like to build a domed structure if the nest box is large enough to permit this. If the nest box is too small or too flat, they make do with an open nest.

The hen starts to build the nest as soon as courtship has begun. It takes her only three to five days to build it. Usually, however, she continues to collect individual items of nesting material when the clutch is already complete and incubation is in full swing. This may, but need not necessarily, be connected with the humidity inside the nest box. That a fairly high humidity is required has already been mentioned.

About five to six days after initial copulation the hen lays her first egg. In many cases she proceeds to incubate immediately afterwards, though sometimes this does not happen until the second or third egg has been laid. A clutch generally consists of four to five eggs. In rare cases the number of eggs may be as low as three or as high as six or seven.

The eggs of all lovebirds are white in color and rounded rather than oval. Depending on the species, the eggs measure 19 to 25 mm in length and are 16 to 19 mm in breadth. Their weight, also depending on species, lies between 3.25 and 4.5 gm.

The eggs are incubated for between twenty-one and twenty-four days, solely by the hen. She usually sits very tight and allows the cock to feed her from his crop. Generally she leaves the nest only once or twice a day to relieve herself, get some exercise, and take a little food and, above all, some water. In individual cases it has been observed that the cock takes over from the hen during her short breaks. This behavior is not common, however, but constitutes an exception.

When the hen starts to incubate after having laid the first egg and a total of five eggs has been produced, the complete incubation period is about thirty days. From the twenty-eighth day onward the hen then has the twin tasks of feeding chicks and incubating eggs. While already looking after tiny chicks she sits on the rest of the eggs. For a short period she has to do two different jobs.

HATCHING AND DEVELOPMENT OF THE YOUNG

As with most birds, tiny young lovebirds break out from their shells with the aid of an "egg-tooth." The latter is a small projection on the top part of the beak, near the tip. Sometimes the hen assists the chicks to a certain extent by carefully pecking at the hole that has been made from the inside.

When the humidity is too low, the eggshell may be too hard and too firm for the young to break it. To prevent such hardening, the nest box can be sprinkled with water from the inside or, alternatively, the humidity in the breeding room can be raised. Some breeders recommend bathing the eggs for a few minutes at three-day intervals from about the twelfth day onward, using water of 38 to 39°C. This method can be successful but must be applied very carefully. First, the embryo breathes through the shell. If the egg is submerged in water and all the pores close, death may result. Secondly, there is a danger that the eggs might break when they are taken out of the nest or put back in again. In addition, the wet eggs cool off much more rapidly.

Often, hatching difficulties are due not to too low a humidity but to a lack of vitality in the parent birds. Weak, sickly birds are paired, too much inbreeding goes on, and the living conditions offered to the birds are inadequate. If the parent birds are strong and healthy, then the young will hatch even at a lower humidity.

On hatching, all young lovebirds look uniformly flesh-colored. They have a sparse-to-dense downy plumage, notably on the top side. They have a whitish to lively red-orange color, depending on the species. After several days the bill, feet, and claws begin to grow darker. They turn brown, gray, or blackish, again depending on species. At about ten days of age an eye-slit appears. Two days later the eyes are entirely open. At roughly the same time a second down starts to sprout on the whole body. Growth of this plumage is complete at sixteen to twenty days, and the color of these feathers is gray, blackish gray, or greenish gray, varying with the species.

At about twenty days the first feathers break through their shafts. These are the head feathers, the wing coverts, and the wing and tail feathers. At the age of twenty-eight days these areas are already well feathered and others begin to close. When the young birds are thirty-five to forty days old the plumage is complete, although the feathers continue to grow. Only at around fifty days have the feathers fully filled out.

By this stage most young lovebirds have already fledged. However, with the exception of the Red-faced, they return to the nest box for the night. Together with their parents, they also disappear into the nest when disturbed or sensing danger.

In fledglings the bill is not yet an intense red but rather more yellowish red with dark markings at the base. In young Peach-faced the beak is not yet of a yellowish horn-color but more orange-brown. Young Gray-heads also have a darker bill than their parents (in whom it is almost white).

GROWING INDEPENDENCE

When the young have left the nest box and are able to fly reasonably securely, they soon start to pick up their own food. At first this will be done playfully; after all, the parents are still making sure the young birds get all they need. The father in particular feeds them very reliably at this stage. Slowly but with increasing skill the young learn to take in their own food, and after about ten to fourteen days (though sometimes as many as twenty) they have become independent.

Occasionally some parent birds start to chase and bite the young before they have become fully independent. In such cases the young birds have to be prematurely separated from their parents. They can be housed with birds whose example encourages them to pick up food. Failing this, they should be fed with a porridge of millet and oat flakes. This cooked soft food is given to them, with a spoon, when it has a temperature of about 35°C (warm to the touch). While a little force may be necessary from time to time, the young soon learn to take the porridge from the spoon.

FIRST MOLT

Under normal circumstances the young lovebirds start molting into adult plumage at the age of three to four months. At five to six months this process is often complete, and the birds then have a much brighter plumage which contrasts quite considerably with the first, duller one. The beak assumes its intense red, or horn-yellow, or silvery white. The blackish spots or striations at its base have disappeared. Feet and claws now show their final gray or bluish gray color and have lost the dark spots. The iris, black at first, now gradually turns brown. The young birds have become adult lovebirds.

Dark markings on the bill are characteristic of the juvenile Peach-faced Lovebird.

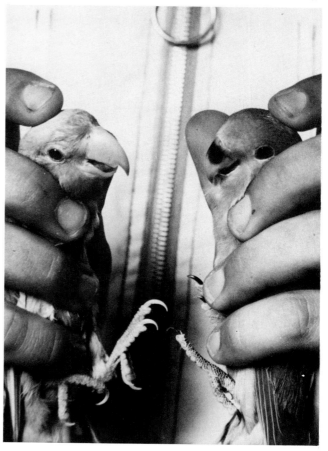

Africa, showing the range
of the Black-collared Lovebird.

Black-collared Lovebird, a mounted
specimen of the nominate race.

Black-collared Lovebird

Agapornis swindernianus **(Kuhl) 1820**
Races: *emini, swindernianus, zenkeri*

DESCRIPTION

Length 13 cm. A green bird with pale green cheeks and underside. A narrow black collar runs round the neck. Below it, the neck is adorned with a yellowish to orange-yellow band which, less distinctly, can also be seen in the throat region. The distal area of back, the rump, and the upper tail-coverts are a deep ultra-navy-blue. Primaries and their coverts are black with green borders, the secondaries and under wing-coverts green. The tail feathers from quill to tip are red, black, and green. Bill black to blackish gray, eyes yellow, feet a dark yellowish green. Cocks and hens are identical in color. Young birds look similar but their colors are duller. The black collar is absent or merely hinted at by a very few black feathers. The bill is pale gray, black at the base. The eyes are brown.

The race *A. s. zenkeri,* known popularly as Zenker's Lovebird or the Cameroons Black-collared Lovebird, was described by Reichenow in 1895 and named after its discoverer G. Zenker. This race is distinguished from the nominate form by a broad reddish brown collar which extends less distinctly to the breast. The race *A. s. emini,* Emin's Lovebird, or the Ituri Black-collared Lovebird, was described in 1908 by Oskar Neumann and named in honor of Emin Pascha, the German explorer whose real name was E. K. O. T. Schnitzer. These birds are slightly bigger, with a deep green plumage. Their beaks are bigger, too, and more strongly curved. The reddish brown area on neck and breast is less extensive than in Zenker's Lovebird.

RANGE AND BEHAVIOR

The race *swindernianus* originates in Liberia. The race *zenkeri* comes from the Cameroons and Gaboon, extending eastward as far as the west of the Central African Republic and Zaire. The race *emini* lives in eastern Zaire and in northwestern Uganda. The ranges of *zenkeri* and *emini* do not appear to border on one another, since Black-collared Lovebirds have not been observed in the Kasai and Mayombe districts.

Black-collared Lovebirds are forest dwellers and spend most of their time high up in the tree-tops. Their presence is given away only by their shrill cries when they fly over the trees in groups of twelve to twenty. Their food is found on the trees. It consists almost exclusively of figs and, above all, their seeds. Black-collared Lovebirds have, however, also been seen in grain fields where they seem to be particularly partial to millet, rice, and corn (the last when the kernels are still milky). The stomach contents of some birds have also revealed grass seeds, fruits, insects and their larvae, and caterpillars. The Black-collared really only come down to the ground to drink, and then only when they cannot find any water in the trees (in leaf fronds or hollow trunks). Of the breeding habits of this species, little is known. The breeding season is said to begin in July or August. The nest is thought to be built in tree cavities and arboreal termitaria.

AVICULTURE

Heinrich Kuhl named the Black-collared Lovebird after the Dutch professor Theodor van Swinderen of Groningen University.

While stuffed specimens have reached Europe, no living birds have so far made it. To date no one outside the birds' native range has succeeded in keeping Black-collared Lovebirds in captivity. Father Hutsebout, a Belgian missionary, kept Black-collareds in their homeland. He said that without fresh figs the birds died within three to four days. He tried to adapt them to millet sprays and other seed but was unsuccessful even when these foods were mixed into the figs.

It can be said, therefore, that the Black-collared as a specialist feeder is unsuitable for a life in captivity. The trouble and cost of having to have fresh figs (in a frozen state) in stock at all times might at best seem manageable by zoological gardens. The responsibility of sacrificing countless numbers of these birds just to be able perhaps to keep a few in the end must seem too great to every animal lover. It is hoped that the Black-collared Lovebirds will be preserved along with the rain forests of Central Africa.

Abyssinian Lovebird cock.

Africa, showing the range of the Abyssinian Lovebird.

Abyssinian Lovebird

Agapornis taranta **(Stanley) 1814**
Races: *nana, taranta*

DESCRIPTION

Length 15 to 16.5 cm. The cock is a green bird with a red forehead, red beak, and a red ring around the brown eyes. The green of lores, sides of the neck, and the throat is a little lighter, as is that of the rump. Remiges and under wing-coverts black to blackish brown, primaries having narrow green borders. Tail feathers green with a broad black bar almost to their tips. The cere is grayish yellow. The green of the hen is a little more dull. Above all the hen is green on the forehead. Her eye-rings, too, are green. Only her bill is red. The colors of young birds are duller still. They, too, have a green forehead. The beak is yellowish brown, blackish at the base, at the tip whitish yellow. The young males grow their first red feathers on the forehead at about three to four months of age. The first molt is completed at about eight to ten months.

Immediately after hatching nestlings are flesh-colored and have off-white downy feathers on the topside. The feet, too, are flesh-colored at first but soon grow dark, and the beak also assumes a brownish color. At eleven days the eyes open. At thirteen days the second downy plumage begins to sprout, although it is not fully developed until the chicks are about twenty to twenty-two days old. These feathers look blackish to begin with, gray when fully grown. The green plumage is already well on the way at four weeks and completed and filled out at about fifty days.

RANGE AND BEHAVIOR

The Abyssinian Lovebird inhabits the highlands of Ethiopia. It owes its scientific name to the Taranta Pass, famous for the magnificent wild beauty of its scenery. There it

Abyssinian Lovebird hen.

occurs in the forests at altitudes of about 1300 to 3200 m—occasionally, however, in lower regions as well, particularly when there are ripe figs to be had for which it seems to have a special liking. The larger nominate form, *A. t. taranta,* occupies the northern part of the range, roughly from Eritrea to Addis Ababa. The smaller race, *A. t. nana,* on the other hand, is found in southern Ethiopia almost as far as the border of Kenya, approximately where the river Omo flows into Lake Rudolf. The forest in these rocky regions consists of junipers and euphorbias, sometimes mixed with acacias and other trees. The Abyssinians have a preference for really high trees, where they feed on fruits, berries, leaf buds, shoots, and bark. They are encountered in small groups of six to ten. More rarely, up to twenty birds gather on one tree. These groups would appear to be aggregations of families, staying together in their area. Despite great mobility, the Abyssinians live in a small area which they practically never leave. It is even said that they always spend the night in the same hollow tree. These tree cavities are usually the nesting sites of woodpeckers, and the Abyssinians not only roost there but also use them for breeding.

Immediately after dawn the Abyssinian Lovebirds fly off in search of food and drinking water. During the flight they emit a high-pitched noise which sounds like *pseep* or *kseek* and is not very loud. The call-note sounds like *tserrk,* and the warning and fear signals are somewhat shriller cries of *creck* and *crick-crick-crick.*

The nest is built in the hollow of a tree. Tucked under her smaller feathers, the hen carries nesting material such as leaves, strips of leaves, grasses, and even small pieces of broken twigs into the nest. The latter is, however, no more than a pad at the bottom of the nesting hollow. The eggs, numbering four or five, are incubated solely by the hen, and twenty-four to twenty-five days elapse before hatching. The young fledge six to seven weeks later. They are fed by both parent birds.

AVICULTURE

Abyssinian Lovebirds did not come to Europe until 1906, when, as reported by K. Neunzig, they were brought to Austria by Italian dealers. From 1923 onward, according to H. Hampe, they were also imported via Great Britain and soon became available everywhere in larger numbers.

At the beginning these lovebirds are fairly shy, but they soon get used to their keeper. Then they turn into watchful, interested, and lively birds which are far from delicate. Because they are high mountain birds, they should not be acclimated to too warm an environment. Losses are rare. Since their voices are quite pleasant to listen to as the birds twitter and sing, and only occasionally contain an element of shrieking, there is no reason why Abyssinians should not be kept in the house. Neighbors are not disturbed by them either, which unfortunately is not the case with some of the other lovebirds.

As regards food, Abyssinians have a special liking for figs (fresh or well-soaked) but are partial to apple and pear slices as well; they also enjoy a mixture of millet and canary seed. Willow twigs are gnawed at too. Trying to adapt them to any other food is a very slow process.

BREEDING

The first breeding success was achieved in 1909 by G. Rambausek in Vienna, as reported in *Gefiederte Welt* (1911, p. 184). In Germany, the first breeder to have had proven success was W. Reitzig in 1924. He managed to raise four young from a clutch of four. In France and Great Britain the first breeding successes were reported in 1925, and in the USA in 1930.

Breeding Abyssinian Lovebirds is not altogether easy. They do not always mate as readily as, say, the Peach-faced and the Masked. Yet it is perfectly simple to differentiate males and females. The biggest obstacle, undoubtedly, is the animosity of these birds toward one another. If a single pair is kept, it may be a long time before the birds proceed to mate. When one of the partners can be exchanged, breeding may be instantly successful. Mutual like and dislike of the partners thus has a much more important role to play with

Abyssinian Lovebirds

regard to the Abyssinian than with any of the other species.

The courtship behavior of the Abyssinian is similar to that of the other lovebirds. The male frequently shakes his head and scratches his head a lot, but he does not display his tail. The female thrusts back her head, a behavior which can also be seen when she wants to be fed. She then emits begging notes similar to those uttered by the young: *trett-trett-trett*. As already mentioned, Abyssinian eggs are incubated for longer than those of the other lovebirds, namely twenty-four to twenty-five days. In the same way, the young take longer to leave the nest *i.e.*, six to seven weeks. After fledging, the young birds continue to be fed by their parents (that is, predominantly the father) for another seven to ten days. Care is required when the young become independent, as they may suddenly be chased, pecked, and seriously, even fatally, injured by the parents. Alternatively, they may sometimes be deserted by their parents before they are ready to feed themselves. They also may be plucked so severely inside the nest box that they grow sore and bloody. In these cases it may be necessary for their keeper to feed them with a spoon, an eyedropper, or a syringe. Birds that have been hand-reared in this way learn to respond to their keeper and can make endearing pets. They do, however, require the full attention and affection of the person they relate to; otherwise they feel lonely and fail to thrive.

The following lovebird hybrids have been produced:

Abyssinian x Masked
Abyssinian x Fischer's
Masked x Abyssinian

Red-faced Lovebird—the cock
can be recognized by the black
and blue on the bend of the wing.

Africa, showing the range
of the Red-faced Lovebird.

Red-faced Lovebird

Agapornis pullarius (Linne) 1758
Races: *pullarius, ugandae*

DESCRIPTION

Length 14 cm. The cock has a bright orange-red forehead, face, and chin; and its upper throat is also of this color. The topside is green, the underside lighter, often with a yellowish sheen. The rump is pale blue; the upper tail-coverts, green. Bend of wing and under wing-coverts are black, the carpal edge of the wing is blue. The remiges are blackish brown with green borders. The tail feathers are yellow in the base, with a big red spot in the middle and a black band. At the tip they are green. The central tail feathers are green all over. The eyes are dark brown, with a narrow whitish, yellowish, or blue ring. The bill is orangy red above and orange to yellowish below. The cere is a light flesh-color. The feet are gray to greenish gray. The female's face is lighter, more yellowish orangy-red. The green of the body plumage is lighter, too. The best differential characteristic is the green, not black, under wing-coverts. The bend of the wing is green as well, as can be seen very clearly in the perching bird. The carpal edge of the wing is yellow, not blue as in the male. Young birds resemble the hen. The face is more yellowish still, likewise the bill. The young males already have black under wing-coverts when they leave the nest (Hampe) or get them soon after (Vriends). Newly hatched chicks are of a light flesh-color and have white fluffy feathers on top. At about twelve days of age, however, they grow a dense, gray downy plumage.

RANGE AND BEHAVIOR

The native range of the Red-faced Lovebird extends from Guinea and Sierra Leone to southwestern Ethiopia, to Uganda and northwestern Angola. The species also occurs on Sao Tome and in the past was found on the islands of Principe and Fernando Poo in the Gulf of Guinea. The race *A. p. pullarius* is distributed from West Africa to the southwestern Sudan and as far as the border between Zaire and Uganda. Further east, *i.e.,* from southwestern Ethiopia and the southwestern Sudan to Ruanda Urundi and the Kigoma district in northwestern Tanzania, we find the race *A. p. ugandae,* the Ugandan Lovebird. In this race the rump is a paler blue or, as sometimes in the hen, of a green color with no more than a touch of blue.

This is the lovebird with the widest range of distribution and the most unusual breeding behavior. It lives in flat country, and in the highlands it occurs at most at altitudes of up to about 1300 m. Its favorite habitat is grassland which is broken up by groups of bushes and trees, notably plantations, the edges of fields, and the areas surrounding human settlements. It is, further, as happy in thornbush and tree savannahs as in less dense forest areas with young trees. The Red-faced Lovebird does not, however, penetrate into the tall, dense rain forest but remains on its periphery and in more open spots near the edge. This means it is rare in the coastal and rain-forest region of West Africa. On the other hand, it is numerous in the flood region of the lower Niger where grassland alternates with rain forest.

The Red-faced Lovebird is most commonly encountered in groups of twelve to twenty birds or in pairs, although fields of ripening millet, corn, barley, and other cereal crops may attract flocks of over 100 birds. With its habit of hanging onto the seed heads of the plants and pulling them down in batches or bending and breaking them, this bird can devastate the fields within a short time. For this reason, the species is persecuted and hunted by the natives in many areas. Consequently the groups of Red-faced Lovebirds which travel vast distances every day in search of food and water are very cautious and anxious. The bulk of their diet consists of a wide variety of seeding grasses, notably *Soghum halepense.* All sorts of fruits, berries, and buds are eaten in addition. A special favorite of Red-faced Lovebirds is figs. In the evening, with much noise, they almost always return to the same trees to rest. There they are said to spend the night hanging upside down from the branches. They have, however, also been observed perching on the branches, asleep. What they never appear to do, on the other hand, is to roost in hollow trees or the nests of other birds.

The breeding behavior of the Red-faced Lovebird is quite extraordinary. Unlike the other lovebirds, it does not breed in tree cavities, the nests of weavers, or under the roofs of houses; instead it burrows into arboreal termitaria (or, more rarely, terrestrial termitaria with their considerable height of 2 to 3 m). What is so astonishing about this is that these burrows are inhabited by termites. While these insects attack all other living creatures that interfere with their territory, they do not in any way disturb the Red-faced Lovebird when it excavates a tunnel of about 5 cm in diameter and 30 cm in length which leads into a breeding chamber. The termitaria consist partly of loam and earth and partly of termite feces and saliva, as well as wood and leaf fragments which have been chewed by the insects and with their saliva mixed to form a very firm building material.

The construction of the burrow is almost exclusively carried out by the hen. The breeding chamber receives very little padding. Only a few strings of bark or leaf are brought in by the female in her plumage and then broken down into very fine shavings. A nest, let alone a domed one, such as the other lovebirds build is unknown to the Red-faced.

Four to six, rarely seven, eggs are laid. These are incubated solely by the hen. The latter is fed by the cock either in or just outside the nest, but she also takes a break once or twice a day when she emerges to relieve herself and to feed. The period of incubation extends twenty-one to twenty-three days. The young fledge at forty to forty-two days. At the age of about four months the young birds show full adult plumage.

AVICULTURE

The Red-faced came to Europe much earlier than any other lovebird. It must have been around 1730 that Red-faced Lovebirds were first imported alive, since E. Albin in his work *A Natural History of Birds* (written between 1731 and 1738) described the species after a living specimen. Long before that, however, Red-faced Lovebirds are said to have been depicted in paintings, *i.e.*, during the reign of Rudolf II in the years 1576 to 1612. Dr. Karl Russ writes that the Red-faced Lovebird was already mentioned (as the "smallest parrot") in 1605, by Clusius. A more detailed account was provided by Dr. W. Neubert from Stuttgart in 1868, describing the first breeding attempts. Here the hen laid the eggs into a nest box while the cock kept watch on the perch outside, chasing away potential intruders, including a parakeet much bigger than himself, namely, the Australian King Parrot. Imports into Europe of Red-faced Lovebirds from different countries of their range are at times very common; but there are also long periods (of years sometimes) during which this species is not imported at all.

In the early stages the birds are very shy and their health is poor. Since, furthermore, most of them will have had their wings clipped before being shipped abroad, it is advisable initially to keep the new imports in a fairly small cage, at room temperature. After three or four months, when they have adapted to our climate and become less shy and their flight feathers have grown again (replacing the clipped feather stumps that should have been pulled out), the birds should be moved to a larger indoor aviary or an in-and-outdoor flight. It must be kept in mind, however, that Red-faced Lovebirds are easily frightened in captivity and may suffer from shock as a result of being caught and handled. In addition, they are far less intelligent than the other species of lovebirds, as it has often been reported that they do not find the way back in from the outdoor flight even after a long period. This is, of course, a serious drawback since it is very important that the birds spend the nights, which can be cold and wet, indoors—which also prevents their being startled by cats and owls. The winter months should be spent in frost-free surroundings, *i.e.,* again indoors.

Toward members of their own species Red-faced Lovebirds tend to behave peaceably. They should not, however, be kept in association with lovebirds of other species, as they may be aggressive toward these. Other birds, such as finches, weavers, and the like, are safe in their company.

BREEDING

It took a very long time for the first successful breeding results to be achieved. This was in about 1900; E. Spille, Osnabruck, reported that one of his pairs managed to raise two young from the first and three young from the second clutch. The birds were said to have bred in an ordinary nest box. This was not made public, however, until 1929 in the book *Vogel ferner Lander* (''Exotic Birds''). As noted by W. de Grahl in his book, C. T. Metzger in Indianapolis had already raised five young each from two clutches in 1893. Further successes were achieved by the same breeders in the years 1905, 1907, and 1910. None of these results were, however, published in special journals or noted and documented elsewhere. For this reason the successful breeding of Red-faced Lovebirds in 1956, by Mr. A. A. Prestwich, secretary of the Avicultural Society of Great Britain, was ac-

claimed as the first success of this kind in the world. The breeding experiments were carried out over a period of several years, with ten to fifteen pairs, in a spacious outdoor aviary which measured 8 x 6 x 2.5 m. Initially the birds were offered blocks of peat, and they duly burrowed into these. In subsequent years they were given barrels of firm, tightly packed leaf-mold. These, too, were used for constructing breeding chambers (always by the females), and eggs were laid inside them. The eggs invariably were infertile, however, despite intensive courtship and copulation. Eventually, on the 5th of October, 1956, a single young bird emerged from one of the breeding chambers. It was fed by the father for a few more days and then appeared fully independent. Regrettably, however, this young bird died as a result of a sudden cold spell.

All this was recorded in detail in the *Avicultural Magazine.* A few more breeding attempts have succeeded since then. Thus Herr Reinhard Blome from Bremen describes (*AZN* 2/75) how he managed to raise young inside a nest box kept at 30° C in a box cage which measured 80 x 60 x 100 cm, at room temperature. He decided on a temperature of 30° C for the nest box because that is the temperature which prevails inside the termitaria. Into the box he put a block of precisely fitting natural peat (pressed peat tends to disintegrate rather too easily). What is very remarkable above all is that Blome advises against breeding the Red-faced Lovebird in an outdoor aviary since the young, who enjoy a high temperature inside the nest box, are in danger of catching a chill when they have fledged. Another observation Blome has made is that the Red-faced immediately moves away from the nest when disturbed by keeper, cats, or other animals instead of disappearing inside it as the other lovebirds do. This can result in the death of eggs or young, particularly when breeding takes place in outdoor aviaries. These detailed breeding reports indicate just how much imagination, observation, and patience are required if a virtually hopeless venture such as this is to succeed against all the odds.

Red-faced Lovebirds are distinguished from the other lovebirds by their much more erect posture. The male utters a fairly quiet but shrill chirping and twittering song, notably during courtship. Then he makes himself taller still and spreads out his short tail, showing the red and black portions of the feathers. He bobs up and down or shakes his head and excitedly runs to and fro on the branch. When mating, the female does not spread out her wings like other lovebirds. During the act of copulation, which lasts several minutes, the female makes whimpering noises.

A clutch generally consists of three to five eggs. In captivity, incubation takes about twenty-four days—slightly longer, it would appear, then in the birds' natural habitat and longer than it takes with other lovebirds. The young also take longer to fledge (six to eight weeks), but once they have left the nest they do not return to it even for the night.

There are no reports about hybrids and mutations so far, although Vriends hints at a mutation that has supposedly been bred in Switzerland. As yet, however, no information of any kind has been forthcoming about this.

Gray-headed Lovebird cock.

Africa, showing the range of the Gray-headed Lovebird.

Gray-headed Lovebird

Agapornis canus **(Gmelin) 1788**
Races: *ablectaneus, canus*

DESCRIPTION

Length 13 to 14 cm. The cock's entire head, neck, chin, throat, and upper breast are whitish gray. Wing-coverts and back are dark green, rump and upper tail-coverts somewhat lighter. The underside is clearly of a lighter, almost yellowish, green. The remiges are blackish brown, the under wing-coverts black, the carpal edge white. The green tail feathers are barred with black above the green tips. The eyes are brown, and the narrow eye-ring is reddish brown. The bill is whitish gray or pinkish white. The feet are pinkish gray to light bluish gray in color. Where the male is whitish gray the female is green, although the head looks slightly brownish. The under wing-coverts are green, rump and upper tail coverts more yellowish. The tail is less distinctly barred. Young birds resemble the hen. They have a yellowish to pinkish yellow bill, with black striations or speckles at the base of the upper mandible. Some young males develop their gray plumage on the head and breast while they are still in the nest. It is said that in the wild the gray feathers do not appear until the first molt at about three to four months. Birds in captivity, on the other hand, are described as having at least a few gray feathers when they fledge. Nestlings are covered in yellowish white fluffy feathers at first. The second downy plumage is gray.

Gray-headed Lovebird hen.

RANGE AND BEHAVIOR

The Gray-headed Lovebird comes from Madagascar. The race *A. c. canus* occurs in the north, west, and east of the island. It is absent only from the central highlands, as well as from the southwest where the race *A. c. ablectaneus* is found. The race *canus* was introduced to Rodriguez, Mauritius, and Reunion (the Macarene Islands), the Comoros, the Seychelles, Zanzibar, and Mafia (Tanzania). Gray-headed Lovebirds are most commonly encountered on the coastal plain. In the mountains they do not go above altitudes of about 1000 m. They love open country with shrubs and well-spaced trees. The dense rain forest is generally avoided by them. Gray-heads are usually seen in groups of five to twenty birds. Occasionally, however, they are said to be observed in flocks of fifty to eighty, particularly where there is a harvest of rice or millet to be had. Their staple diet consists of grass seeds which they gather almost exclusively from the ground. Here they are frequently found in association with the Madagascar Weaver *(Foudia madagascariensis)* and the Bib Finch (*Lonchura nana*). Persecution, due to the damage caused in the fields, has turned them into fairly shy and wary birds. Their flight is quick and direct, although they are well able to make their way through the trees. In flight they emit shrieking calls which are not, however, all that loud. On other occasions a quite pleasant twittering can be heard. The males may even utter a chattering song (particularly during courtship) which bears some resemblance to that of the Budgerigar and the Abyssinian Lovebird.

The nest is built in a hollow tree. The hen generally makes a pad from strips of leaves, grass, bark, and seed pods. She carries the material to the nest in small pieces tucked under her plumage, using for this purpose not only the feathers of rump and back but also those of neck, breast, and sides. When she has tucked away about thirty items she flies to the nest, dropping a good many of them on the way. The number of eggs laid usually totals three or four, although there may sometimes be as many as five or six. The eggs are incubated by the female for about eighteen to twenty-two days. The cock assists in the feeding of the nestlings.

AVICULTURE

A painting by Brisson dating as far back as 1760 depicts a Gray-headed Lovebird, as W. de Grahl reports. London Zoo received a pair in 1860. From 1880, when Hagenbeck imported them in large numbers, until just before World War II these birds were sold in a great many pet shops. Then Madagascar imposed a general export embargo which was not lifted until fairly recently and then only on a few occasions.

Gray-headed Lovebirds need to be acclimated at temperatures of about 22 to 24° C; otherwise they are prone to chills and may die of pneumonia. Once they have gotten used to our climate they cease to be over-delicate and can thrive and be happy at a lower temperature, provided it does not fall below the freezing point. They spend the night inside a nest box, which affords them additional protection from the cold.

Indoor-outdoor connecting aviaries are really the only type of accommodation that is suitable for birds with such a strong urge for movement. Indeed, while being alert, lively, and full of curiosity in an aviary and soon losing all fear, when kept in a cage they display a dull, shy behavior and constantly utter anxious croaking sounds. If a cage is to be used, it must not house more than one pair since in this environment the birds become aggressive toward members of their own and, above all, those of other species. In a spacious aviary, on the other hand, they are fairly peaceable birds.

Gray-headed Lovebirds kept on their own have become hand-tame and even learned to talk.

BREEDING

Dr. Karl Russ, in 1872, was the first to succeed in breeding the Gray-headed Lovebird. His success was soon followed by reports of the same achievement by other breeders and in other countries. The propagation of this species is never easy, even if in a few isolated cases it has actually succeeded in a cage. It depends entirely on how tame the breeding birds are, whether a quiet, secluded spot has been provided for their nest box, and whether the keeper is able to prevent the pair from being disturbed in any way. Nest inspection is generally resented and may lead to desertion of eggs or young.

Budgerigar nest boxes of horizontal design are more readily accepted than vertical (de Grahl). Into this box the hen carries a varying amount of nesting material such as pieces of leaf and twig, the needles of pines or larches, strips of bark, and so on. The nesting material is tucked under the plumage and shaken off inside the nest box. Some females do not collect any nesting material at all. It is, therefore, advisable to line the boxes with a layer of peat fibers, wood shavings, and/or old larch- and pine-needles before hanging them up.

During courtship the male trips around the female, bobbing excitedly and singing nonstop. Apart from that, there are no differences from the courtship behavior of the other lovebirds. The hen is often seen hanging just outside the entrance to the nest box, with a fanned tail and jerking wings. In this way she indicates that she is ready to mate, as well as pointing out which nest box she has chosen.

The eggs are incubated solely by the female. The male feeds her regularly and when doing so often spends a considerable time in the nest box. During the period of incubation the cock sleeps in a different nest box, which is another reason for providing several boxes. The male does his share of feeding the young, and when they have fledged he becomes solely responsible for providing them with food, since often by that time the hen already has another clutch. The young birds continue to return to their nest for a long while and do not become independent until three weeks after fledging. From then on it is possible that they may be chased away and bitten by the father.

Hybridization with other lovebirds has so far not occurred. As related by Karl Neunzig, cross-breeding between a Gray-headed Lovebird and a Budgerigar is said to have taken place among the stock of Baron von Grote in 1890. A report on this case can be found in *Gefiederte Welt* (1890, p. 223). The hybrid is described as having the markings of a Budgerigar but the silver-gray head, neck, and upper breast of a Gray-headed male.

Mutations are unknown in the Gray-headed Lovebird.

Outdoor aviaries are the most suitable accommodation for lovebird breeding colonies.

45

Normal Peach-faced Lovebird.

Africa, showing the range
of the Peach-faced Lovebird.

Peach-faced Lovebird

Agapornis roseicollis **(Vieillot) 1818**
Races: *roseicollis, catumbella*

DESCRIPTION

Length 16 to 18 cm. Color of the head, to as far as behind the eyes, an attractive pinkish red. Chin, throat, and upper breast of the same color. Back of the head, neck, back, and wing-coverts grass-green to lime-green; underside paler, more yellowish green. Rump and upper tail-coverts a bright light-blue color. The remiges are blackish with green borders. The tertial feathers are green, likewise the under wing-coverts. The central tail feathers are green, the remainder bearing a big, bright pinkish-red to orange-red spot, below which on the inner web there is a black spot. All tail feathers are blue at the tip. The eyes are dark brown and surrounded by a narrow white or yellowish ring. The cere is flesh-colored, the bill the yellowish color of horn, with a greenish tinge along the edges and (often) a greenish black tip. The feet are gray, greenish gray or bluish gray, the claws brown to black. In birds of the race *A. r. catumbella* the pinkish red parts of the face are brighter still. Likewise, the green of their plumage is stronger, too. Hen and cock are extremely difficult to distinguish. The hen is slightly bigger but has a smaller, rounder head. Her pinkish red color is

A group of fully-colored Peach-faced Lovebirds.

paler and less widespread. The pinkish red of the tail is paler, less extensive, and less well defined. There are, however, females with stronger colors than those of some males. In the same way, some hens may be smaller than unusually large males. The best differentiating characteristic is the greater pelvic width of the hen. Usually, however, this difference can be discerned only in fully grown birds. In juveniles the red face mask is paler, the green plumage more grayish and dull.

Nestlings are flesh-colored and have orange-red fluff on the upper side. Bill and feet are light-colored. They grow dark at about ten days of age, the bill becoming quite black; the eyes begin to open and the downy feathers to sprout. The latter soon cover the whole bird and are dark gray in color, although some of them may be yellowish green at first.

RANGE AND BEHAVIOR

The home of the Peach-faced Lovebird is Namibia and southwestern Angola. The race *A. r. catumbella* is found in the northernmost part of the range, in the area around the port of Benguela. Peach-faced Lovebirds are generally encountered in groups of ten to twelve birds. Their flight is very fast and direct, making them virtually impossible to identify. All the time they are on the wing, however, they utter fairly loud and shrill calls. The habitat of this species consists of dry steppes and savannahs from the lowlands to altitudes of 1600 m. There one usually finds only a few groups of trees and shrubs, proper forests being rare. Of vital importance to the Peach-faced is the proximity of water. This is generally visited twice a day: in the morning and late afternoon.

The breeding behavior of the Peach-faced is very interesting. The birds breed in colonies. Very extensive, domed nests may be built inside rock crevices or under the roofs of houses. Most commonly, however, Peach-faced Lovebirds breed in the nesting colonies of the Sociable Weaver *(Philetairus socius)* and the nests of the Stripe-breasted Sparrow-Weaver *(Plocepasser mahali)*. The nests of these weavers are usually located in large acacias. While the Sociable Weavers hang their pear-shaped nests very close together on the branches, the Sparrow-Weavers actually build a communal nest with many breeding chambers. Such a nest can have a diameter of up to 7 m and be 3 m thick. Inside it are the many individual nests of the weavers. Now the Peach-faced Lovebirds have chosen these nests for raising their young. Not content with moving into empty nests, they even select nests that are still occupied.

When adopting weavers' nests the Peach-faced gather hardly any nesting material at all. If, however, they build their own nest in rock crevices, hollow trees, or under roofs, they carry under the rump feathers strips of bark, grass blades, and shreds of palm leaves into the nest. It is the hen who is responsible for building the nest. The males are passive in this respect, merely flying to and fro with the females.

AVICULTURE

The first Peach-faced Lovebirds were imported in about 1860, by Karl Hagenbeck. Since then they have been available at fairly regular intervals, with the exception of the war years when they were rather scarce. Because the Peach-faced proved easy to breed, they were soon propagated in sufficient numbers in this country. Today they are the most commonly kept and most numerous of the lovebirds.

The Peach-faced are very easy to acclimate. They are hardy and resistant. During the period of acclimation they should be kept in cages or small aviaries at a temperature of about 20°C. Within three months they will have become so well adapted that they can be allowed out into garden aviaries if it happens to be spring or summer. Nowadays almost all the Peach-faced that come on the market have been bred in captivity. This means, of course, that the birds have been used to our climate for many generations and may be left outside in the garden aviary all year 'round. Only during severe frost should they remain indoors since their feet are prone to frostbite, particularly as a result of holding onto the wire mesh.

Unfortunately the Peach-faced have two faults without which they would be even more

Lutino Peach-faced Lovebird.

popular. One of these is their aggressive nature. This is directed against all birds, whether they are members of the same species or whether they are smaller or larger. Among Peach-faces themselves fierce fighting takes place, while birds of other species usually get bitten on the legs. It is preferable, therefore, to keep the Peach-faced in pairs. Anyone wishing to keep a flock of these birds in a very spacious aviary should introduce the birds to each other while they are still quite young. Then they usually all get on reasonably well together.

The other shortcoming of Peach-faced lovebirds is that the more of them that are housed together, the more loudly and persistently do they utter their shrill cries. These are repetitive noises sounding like *shreek-shreek-shreek*. Even a single pair can make a nuisance of itself in this way if kept in an apartment. A lone bird, on the other hand, frequently almost stops calling altogether, particularly if it was separated from other members of its species at a very early age. Nevertheless it is not advisable to keep a single Peach-faced Lovebird. While the bird is likely to become fairly tame, it will show little ability to learn to talk.

BREEDING

The first breeding success was achieved in 1869 at Berlin Zoo. The director, A. E. Brehm, described this in detail in *Brehms Tierleben* ("Brehm's Animal Life"). Arousing a lot of interest at the time was the fact that the Peach-faced Lovebirds carry under their rump feathers nesting material in the form of chewed strips of bark. As already mentioned earlier, the females collect the nesting material while the males merely accompany them on their flights. In the nest the nesting material is shaken out of the rump feathers and worked into the structure. The nest often becomes quite large. The entrance to the breeding chamber lies toward the back of the nest box. For the purpose of nest inspection it will therefore be an advantage if the back wall of the nest box can be taken off. Important, too, is that the nest box be not too small. It must have an inside bottom of at least 16 x 16 cm and a height of 25 cm. The walls of the nest

box should consist of wooden boards of no less than 2 cm thickness.

Mating behavior is similar to that seen in lovebirds with white eye-rings. The partners trip to and fro on the branches. The cock flies around the hen in narrow semi-circles, landing first on her right and then on her left. A lot of feeding goes on. The male also does a lot of calling, and both partners repeatedly scratch themselves on the head. For the act of copulation the hen crouches, extending her wings, cocking her tail, and bending back her raised head.

The first egg is laid just a few days after the initial copulation. Thereafter an additional egg is laid every other day until there is a clutch of three to five or, more rarely, six to seven. Often the hen starts to incubate when only the first egg has been produced. Sometimes incubating does not begin until the second or third egg is lying in the nest. During the incubation period the hen is fed by the cock. A few times each day, however, she emerges from the nest box to look for food and to relieve herself. The eggs are incubated for twenty-one to twenty-three days.

It is not entirely unusual where the Peach-faced Lovebird is concerned for eggs to die. One reason for this is too low a humidity in the breeding room, or it may be caused by weak and sickly parent birds which are probably too closely related. The humidity should be at least 60%. This can be achieved by spraying water (from a dispenser) into the air, spraying the nest box, using an electric humidifier, and by constantly providing fresh nesting material, particularly in the form of willow twigs. In bird houses with a cement floor the latter can be kept damp during the breeding season. If the nest boxes are hung up in garden aviaries, out in the open and on the shady side, they should usually be damp enough inside.

The young, covered in orange-red fluff, are fed predominantly by the female at first but later increasingly by the male as well. They begin to see when they are ten days old and the second downy plumage is starting to grow. These feathers are grayish green, although yellowish in the early stages. At about twenty days the tips of the wing and tail feathers begin to emerge. By the time the birds fledge, at thirty-eight to forty-two days, almost all the large feather are fully grown.

The young birds continue to be fed conscientiously by the parent birds, notably the father, for another ten to fourteen days after fledging. Then they are independent and are frequently chased off and bitten, since the parents may already have started a second brood. When several pairs breed in the same aviary, great care is required on the keeper's part when the young have fledged. If the young birds get too close to the territory—let alone the nest box—of one of the other adult pairs, they will be attacked and in many cases severely injured. Sometimes losses among the young birds have been caused by strange adult birds.

There are records of hybridization of the Peach-faced with the following species:

Peach-faced x Masked
Peach-faced x Fischer's
Peach-faced x Nyasa
Peach-faced x Black-cheeked
Masked x Peach-faced
Fischer's x Peach-faced
Nyasa x Peach-faced
Black-cheeked x Peach-faced

MUTATIONS

A recessive Yellow mutation occurred in Japan in 1954. The breeder of this mutation was Masuru Iwata from Nagoya. He called it *Rozakura,* which means "Golden Cherry Lovebird". The first of these Golden Cherries to come to Europe were kept by Dr. Burkard of Zurich, in 1967. Although repeatedly imported, the Golden Cherry still remains fairly rare in Europe. Furthermore, these birds have been crossed with the other yellow mutation, which has resulted in considerable confusion. Today we can see yellow Peach-faced Lovebirds in a wide range of colors—from the beautiful canary-yellow of the Golden Cherry, with its intensely red face and blue rump, to the pale yellow and greenish yellow birds with a yellow-orange face and a yellowish gray rump. As opposed to the wild color, the inheritance of Golden Cherry is recessive (see Table 4).

Another yellow mutation, resulting from a recessive factor, first appeared in South Africa, in the stock of Mr. H. H. Parker, who described it in the September 1957 issue of *Birds Monthly Illustrated.* It all began when he found a bird with only a few yellow feathers among his stock which after the molt turned out to be a magnificent yellow female. He bred it with a cock which also had just a few yellow feathers, and all the young produced by this pair were of the normal (green) color. When a male from this generation was bred with his mother, again only green youngsters were produced. Now a grandchild was mated to the yellow female, but again only green offspring were produced. One of these young birds, however, changed into a splendid, intense yellow during the molt. The face is of a paler red than in wild-colored birds. The young are invariably green until their first molt, even if Yellow is bred with Yellow. (For the recessive inheritance of this mutation, see Table 4.)

The Pied mutation of the Peach-faced first appeared in the early 1960s in California. The contrast between intense green and bright yellow areas of plumage is often quite marked, making the birds look very handsome indeed. In some of these individuals, however, lighter patches appear among the green and the changeover to yellow is not too distinct. Such birds are not very attractive. Care should also be taken not to cross in other color variations as this, too, tends to result in less attractive pieds. Because the Pied factor is a dominant one, it is really quite easy to breed this mutation. The breeder has, of course, little influence on the distribution of the colors over the bird's body. Even when both parents are very similar and the yellow is distributed over about 50% of the plumage, the offspring will not necessarily show the same color arrangement. In fact, their markings may be entirely different, either containing little yellow or with yellow predominating. It is this high degree of unpredictability that makes the breeding of pieds so extremely interesting. Table 1 illustrates the inheritance of the Pied factor and thus applies to pied greens among the Peach-faced Lovebirds.

According to M. Vriends, Blue Peach-faced were first bred by P. Habats in Holland in

1963. Unlike, for instance, the Blue Masked, they are, however, not a bright blue color but rather more bluish green or sea-green, barely turquoise. The throat is often whitish in these birds, the forehead light orange. In spite of its less attractive blue, this color variety became the most common one everywhere in Europe. Its inheritance is recessive and Table 3 applies.

The Lutino Peach-faced originated in the U.S.A. According to W. de Grahl, a single bird came to England in 1942 but died before reaching its destination. Further Lutinos (according to Dr. Erhard, *AZN* 8/75) were bred in 1969 by Mrs. Schertzer in San Diego, California. She gave a young Lutino bird to Dr. Erhard, himself a resident of the U.S.A., in 1973. Having been told by Mrs. Schertzer that the Lutino factor was recessive, Dr. Erhard was able to establish its sex-linkage (see Table 8).

The Dark-green and Olive Peach-faced originally occurred in Australia. When exactly they first appeared there unfortunately I do not know. The first specimens to be sent from Australia to Europe were received by Dr. R. Burkard of Zurich in 1972. This mutation is the result of intermediate inheritance where the combined effect of the wild color and a dark factor (either single or double) produces the colors Dark-green and Olive (see Table 2).

Yellow-blue Peach-faced Lovebirds are an example of combining mutations. They occur among the offspring of Pied Green x Blue. As with yellow-green pieds, the color distribution can show a great deal of variation. Usually, however, breast, underside, under tail-coverts, back, wing-coverts, and rump are of a light-blue or turquoise color, whereas forehead, crown, the carpal edges of the wings, and the tail feathers are yellow. The bill often has a somewhat orangy or horn color in these birds.

Another color variety resulting from the combination of two mutations are blue-white birds. According to Dr. Erhard, these have been produced by pairing Golden Cherry x Blue. The birds concerned are of a rather pale blue and a white or grayish white color, with just a touch of pale pink on the forehead.

A whole host of other combinations have

The name recommended by The African Lovebird Society for this mutation of the Peach-faced Lovebird is *Dark Green*. Called "Olive" in the text, this mutation, which produces a much darker green than the Normal, involves a dark factor which in its single form produces *Medium Green* ("Dark Green") birds. Present as a double dark factor, it produces Dark Green birds. The dark factor can also be transmitted to Dutch Blue and other colors, such as Cinnamon. For the inheritance of this interesting mutation, see Table 2.

been bred, but many of these Peach-face Lovebirds have unattractive colors. Th yellow-white pieds can be quite appealing, pro vided (and this applies to all color mutation: definite color distinctions and pure colors hav been maintained.

Red-pied Peach-faced Lovebirds are not th

This photograph shows another *Dark Green* Peach-faced Lovebird next to a *Dutch Blue* specimen. Only one Blue mutation has occurred in the Peach-faced, in Holland—hence the name Dutch Blue. Comparisons with the photo on the left and birds shown on subsequent pages indicate the wide variations possible in Peach-faced mutations.

The *American Pied Light Greens* are the most popular breeding and show birds among the Peach-faced. Not all of them have such beautiful, intense colors as the bird in this photograph. In some specimens the colors look rather dilute and the markings are unsightly.

esult of a mutation but occur through modification. It has been shown that the red-ied plumage springs from some nutritional eficiency or perhaps lack of daylight. If such ied birds receive a good diet and adequate ght, they will regain their green color after e next molt. As mentioned by Curt af

Enehjelm in the 1957 edition of Hampe's book on lovebirds, the South African breeder H. H. Parker bred two completely red birds from yellow Peach-faceds. Further details were not available to Enehjelm at the time, and to date we have heard nothing more about any red Peach-faced Lovebirds.

In the Yellow varieties of the Peach-faced Lovebird, the plumage looks yellowish green rather than yellow. The rump is pale bluish to white. Since Yellow mutations have occurred in different places, they are distinguished by adding the name of the country of origin: e.g., *American Yellow*. For the inheritance of these recessive mutations, see Table 4.

This beautiful canary-yellow Peach-faced Lovebird resembles the description given of the *Japanese Yellow* variety, the famous Golden Cherries. However, in the Yellow mutations the rump does not show as intense a blue as this specimen. As evidenced by the markings on the wings, this bird is an *American Pied Light Green*.

This *American Pied Light Green* specimen offers another illustration of the variations in coloration possible with this mutation. For the inheritance of this factor, see Table 1.

The purest yellow is found in *Lutino* Peach-faced Lovebirds. Suprisingly, the inheritance of the Lutino factor is sex-linked in the Peach-faced but recessive in the other lovebird species; see Table 8.

The *Dutch Blue* Peach-faced has become the most common mutation. The blue shows a tremendous variation and never succeeds in looking as colorful and intense as it does in the Blue Masked Lovebird. In the Peach-faced it may be a bluish green, sea green, or turquoise shade, and some parts of the body (face and throat) come out yellowish. For the inheritance of the Blue factor, see Table 3.

American Pied Dutch Blue Peach-faced are very often seen nowadays. Their blue, not as pure and bright as that of the Blue Masked Lovebird, is best described as turquoise. While the Pied factor is dominant to the Normal, the Blue factor is recessive; Tables 1 and 3 explain this color variety.

On first glance, this bird might be thought to be a Pied Green. If it were, however, its face ought to be red. Since the face is lighter than the body, this is an *American Pied Dutch Blue*. This combination is produced by Pied Green x Blue.

American Pied Dutch Blue. This specimen is the result of selective pairings among American Pied Dutch Blues. When breeding these birds a great deal of patience is required, as is a fair-sized stock of birds with good colors.

The *Lutino* Peach-faced are a magnificent yellow and an intense red, which also persists in the tail feathers. The rump is white with a very faint blue sheen. The feet are flesh-colored. The red eyes are more obvious in direct illumination, and Lutino nestlings are immediately recognizable by their light eyes visible through the skin. Their skin seems lighter too, and the reddish down is very sparse and present only on the upper side.

Dutch Blue Ino, formerly called "Cream" or "Albino." This sex-linked color variety can be produced by pairing Lutino x Blue. The result is very interesting birds of an attractive, almost whitish color. To produce Dutch Blue Inos, two generations are required. First of all, Lutino cocks are mated with Blue hens. The resultant young males are Normal, split for Blue and Lutino. The young hens are Lutinos split for Blue. In pairing these birds a very small percentage of Dutch Blue Ino young will be achieved.

This specimen is a combination of Dutch Blue and one of the Yellow mutations. If it is the American Yellow, then the variety is properly called *American White*. As Yellows have often been called Cherryheads, "Silver Cherry," or simply "Silver" has been used to designate this variety. In England it has been called "Buttermilk."

American Pied White can be created by crossing a Yellow of American origin with a Pied Dutch Blue. The nestlings have white down and plum-colored eyes. No red is visible on the tail feathers. Cheeks and throat are whitish gray, the wings white to light gray. Tables 1, 3, and 4 apply.

Dutch Blue Peach-faced Lovebird (photo
San Diego Zoo).

Dutch Blue Ino Peach-faced Lovebird.

American Yellow Peach-faced Lovebird
(photo San Diego Zoo).

American White Peach-faced Lovebird.

American Pied Light Green Peach-faced Lovebird.

American Pied Dutch Blue Peach-faced Lovebird.

Black-cheeked Lovebird

Agapornis nigrigenis **Sclater 1906**

DESCRIPTION

Length 14 to 15 cm. Forehead and crown a reddish black-brown; lores, chin, throat, and cheeks brownish black to sooty black. The back of the head and the neck are a darkish olive-green. Throat yellow to orange-red. Remainder of plumage green, more intense above than below. Rump and upper tail-coverts green as in the Nyasa Lovebird. Tail green, outer feathers having black bars and orange-red spots in the center of the vane. Eye-rings and the narrow cere white. Bill red, base of upper mandible light-red to pink. Eyes brown, feet gray to flesh-colored, claws light brown. The female's coloration is similar, except that the plumage on the cheeks is often less black and more brownish as well as being less glossy; and the forehead is less reddish brown, the neck not olive but rather more green. The throat spot tends to be smaller and paler. In addition, the female is slightly bigger and has a smaller and rounder head. The hen's iris is said to be browner than the cock's. Juveniles have duller colors altogether. They have darker claws and usually dark spots or striations on the beak and feet. The nestlings are flesh-colored and bear orange-colored down. The second down, which begins to sprout at twelve days of age, is grayish green.

RANGE AND BEHAVIOR

This species occurs in the southwesternmost part of Zambia, *i.e.,* from the Kafue National Park to the Victoria Falls and eastward in the Zambezi valley to as far as the northeastern tip of Namibia and the western tip of Zimbabwe where the four countries meet at Razungula on the Zambezi. There Black-cheeked Lovebirds live mainly along the wooded river banks at an altitude of about 600 m, or in slightly higher regions (up to about 1300 m above sea level). They can be observed in small flocks of twelve to twenty birds, flying along—with not too much noise—in a straight line and at considerable speed. Notably in the mornings and late in the afternoons they come to the watering places. Otherwise they are rarely seen on the ground, since they normally feed perched in the trees or on grasses. They live on a wide variety of seeds, especially grass seeds, millet and other cereal crops, and on fruit, berries, leaf buds, and blossoms. Little is known about their breeding cycle in the wild, but they are said to build their domed nests in hollow trees, in the nests of weavers, and under the roofs of huts. Nesting material consists mainly of strips of palm fronds, although the birds also use strips of bark from various broad-leaved trees. In all other respects the behavior of Black-cheeked Lovebirds is identical to that of the other species with white eye-rings.

AVICULTURE

The first Black-cheeked Lovebirds came to Europe as early as in 1907, one year after Sclater described them. As reported by Neunzig, Fockelmann of Hamburg imported a larger number of this species in 1908, and the birds soon became very popular. They proved

66

to be equally happy in a cage, birdroom, or garden aviary.

Freshly imported Black-cheeked Lovebirds should be acclimated at room temperature. In the winter they should be kept in a moderately heated indoor aviary. However, since a strict embargo has been imposed on the export of these birds from their native habitat, all birds currently for sale will have been bred in captivity.

Opinions vary as to how peace-loving the Black-cheeked is. Outside the breeding season the birds are fairly peaceable among themselves, particularly when they have been housed together from their early days. They are sometimes aggressive toward newcomers. On the whole they get along well with other species such as weavers, cardinals, starlings, and sometimes Budgerigars and Cockatiels. They can be kept in a cage if it is a spacious one. A pair may then become very tame. A single bird may even sit on one's finger and grow as affectionate as a Budgerigar. (To achieve this, however, it would have to associate solely with humans from the moment it becomes independent.) Ideally the birds should be kept in pairs in small outdoor aviaries which give access to frost-free indoor compartments.

BREEDING

The Black-cheeked Lovebird was first bred in Britain by Mr. R. Phillips in 1908. In Germany the pioneer was Frau J. Prove. Her first brood hatched on September 26, 1908. In the U.S.A., too, it was a woman who achieved the first successful result with these birds, namely, Mrs. Thompson, in 1909. At first the cultivation of the Black-cheeked seemed to flourish. By 1925, however, those in human hands had more or less died out. A year later new wild catches were reaching the breeders so that stocks were able to recover. Toward the end of the fifties, however, the Black-cheeked had once again become so rare in cages and aviaries that their continued existence seemed in doubt. Further exports from their country of origin were prohibited since the birds had become scarce in their natural habitat as well,

and their range is a fairly narrow one. If man had continued to catch and export them, they would have faced possible extinction. (In one month in 1926, for example, 16,000 Black-cheeked were caught and exported, the main reason being the extensive damage they had been causing to millet and other cereal crops. This is reported by Dr. Vriends.) Today there exist small stocks of Black-cheeked Lovebirds which unfortunately are often interbred with the Masked. This should obviously be avoided, since back-crossing is difficult and tedious and therefore to be considered only as a last resort.

Breeding the Black-cheeked causes few if any problems. Wherever possible, each pair should have its own garden aviary. Courtship, nest building, egg laying, incubation, and rearing of the young are the same as for the other lovebirds with white eye-rings.

Hybrids have been produced with the following species:

Black-cheeked x Masked
Black-cheeked x Fischer's
Black-cheeked x Nyasa
Black-cheeked x Peach-faced
Masked x Black-cheeked
Fischer's x Black-cheeked
Nyasa x Black-cheeked
Peach-faced x Black-cheeked

Hybridization with Budgerigars is said to have occurred also, but such reports should be treated with caution.

MUTATIONS

Due to the small stocks of Black-cheeked, only Yellow (yellowish green) and Blue mutations have been bred—via the Masked, of course. That is, we are concerned with hybrids of the F_1 or, at most the F_2 generation. If sufficient numbers of Black-cheeked homozygous for wild color (without a trace of blue on the rump) were available, the establishment of the Blue and Yellow mutations would present no difficulties whatsoever. Both mutations are subject to recessive inheritance (see Tables 3 and 4).

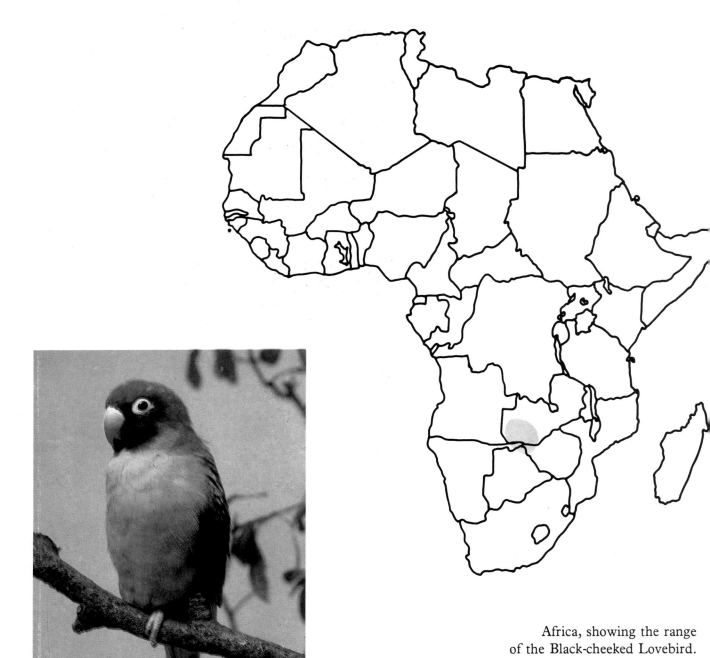

Black-cheeked Lovebird.

Africa, showing the range
of the Black-cheeked Lovebird.

The Yellow Masked Lovebird (right) is the source of yellow in Black-cheeked Lovebirds. The color is more yellowish green than yellow. Below: Black-cheeked Lovebird, normal coloration (photo by M. Vriends).

Nyasa Lovebird

Agapornis lilianae **Shelley 1894**

DESCRIPTION

Length 13 to 14 cm. Head (to as far as beyond the eyes), chin, and throat strawberry-red. Back of head, neck (including the sides) light olive-green. The remaining plumage a strong green color. Under tail-coverts, rump, and upper tail-coverts a somewhat lighter green. Tail feathers, to as far as the tip, bluish on the upper sides. The narrow cere and eye-rings white. Eyes dark brown, bill an intense red, feet gray, bluish gray or more flesh-colored tinged with gray. Male and female are of the same coloration. In the hen the red color tends to be slightly paler and less luminous, however. Apart from that, the sex differences are as described with regard to the other species with white eye-rings. In juveniles all the colors are less bright, and up to the age of three to four months the claws are darker, while the bill is yellowish red with a touch of black at the base of the upper mandible. Nestlings have a flesh-colored skin and are covered in salmon-covered down with a slight touch of gray. The second down is light to darkish gray-green.

RANGE AND BEHAVIOR

This species is found from southwestern Tanzania and northwestern Mozambique southwestward through Malawi and the eastern half of Zambia to as far as northern Rhodesia. It loves the lower terrain at altitudes of 300 to 1600 m where it occurs especially along river valleys and the shores of lakes. The Nyasa Lovebird is particularly common in the Lake Nyasa area as well as along the banks of the central Zambezi and the Luangwa. The bird occurs mainly in mopane woods but also in acacias. Outside the breeding season the species is fairly sociable and travels in flocks of twenty to over 100 birds. In flight the birds utter their shrill, if not very loud, calls. They fly quickly and in a straight line. Several times a day they go off in search of water. When feeding, too, they are frequently encountered on the ground where they look principally for grass seeds. In the trees they feed on seeds, fruit, leaf buds, and blossoms. Acacia blossoms are said to be part of their diet, too. When the cereal crops ripen, notably millet, the Nyasas like to raid the fields.

During the beginning of the breeding season, which lasts from December to March or April, the flocks split up into smaller groups. The birds then look for suitable breeding holes in the trees. They also breed in the deserted nests of Buffalo Weavers, however, and even under the roofs of huts and houses. The nesting material—consisting of thin twigs, the chewed juicy bark of various trees, and above all strips of palm fronds—is carried by the hen in her bill into the nest hole and structured into a complex domed nest.

AVICULTURE

In 1864, Kirk discovered the Nyasa Lovebirds by the Shire River in Nyasaland (now known as Malawi). He mistook them for Peach-faced Lovebirds, however. Because of this, they were not named and described until 1894, by Shelley. The specific name *lilianae* was chosen by Shelley in honor of Lilian, the sister of the famous British ornithologist Philip Lutley Sclater (1829-1913). The first importation of the Nyasa did not come about for a long time, however. The first birds of this species eventually came to Britain in 1926. In the same year Mr. Stokes in Britain, Mme. Lecallier in France, and R. Neunzig in Germany succeeded in the first breeding of the Nyasa Lovebirds (also initially mistaking them for Peach-faced). During the early years in captivity the Nyasa were considered the most prolific of all the lovebirds and the easiest to propagate. As a result of World War II and the hard times that followed it, stocks shrank considerably. Due to export embargos imposed by Malawi and other countries where the Nyasas are native and because of the import ban on all parrots here, the few existing birds were subjected to excessive inbreeding as well as being cross bred with the Peach-faced. The consequence of this was that Nyasa Lovebirds in the care of humans had almost disappeared, and successful breeding attempts were very rare. There was a slight improvement in the situation in the sixties and early seventies when a few birds were allowed to be exported. Successful breeding became a reality again, but even today the Nyasa remains the rarest of all the lovebirds with white eye-rings.

Acclimation of imported Nyasas is not easy. They are weak at first. Presumably the adaptation to new kinds of food is difficult for them since many of the birds quite suddenly die of enteric infections. Metabolic disturbances, and consequently inflammations of the liver, are also more common in this than in other species. After acclimation at room temperature Nyasa Lovebirds may be left in the garden aviaries from spring to late fall. Some sort of shelter or an indoor aviary should be available to the birds at all times. It is better not to let them spend the winter outside but to provide them with a moderately heated indoor birdroom. Apart from aviaries, biggish cages are another possible type of accommodation for this species. Nyasa Lovebirds are fairly sociable and peaceable among themselves. Several pairs therefore may be kept in one aviary. They are not aggressive toward other species of birds either and so can be kept in company with larger finches and weavers, Budgerigars and Cockatiels, and doves and quails.

BREEDING

Breeding succeeds whether several pairs are kept in a spacious garden aviary, or a single pair in a correspondingly smaller aviary or a cage which measures approximately 100 x 60 x 50 cm. Wherever possible, each pair should be offered a choice of two nest boxes. They seem to have a preference for upright boxes with an inner base of 14 x 14 cm and a height of 20 to 25 cm. The entrance hole should measure 5 cm in diameter.

Courtship behavior is similar to that of the other lovebirds with white eye-rings. Prior to mating the male seems to scratch his head even more frequently than do males of the other species. Nest building is the female's task: she chews off strips of bark from willows, poplars, lindens, and other broad-leaved trees and carries them into the nest box in her bill. Blades of grass, the stalks of chickweed, and even empty millet sprays are incorporated into the nest as well.

About a week after first mating the female lays the first egg. Every other day another egg is added until the clutch of four to five eggs is complete. Only the hen incubates. The cock usually accompanies her when she builds the nest. He also spends the night in the nest box with her. The period of incubation spans twenty-one to twenty-three days. Every other day one of the chicks hatches. Despite the considerable differences in size, all the young are looked after very well by the hen. Soon the cock feeds them too, after initially confining himself to feeding the hen while she sits on the chicks and keeps them warm. The development of the young is similar to that seen in the progeny of other lovebirds with white eye-rings. The young birds fledge at about thirty-five days of age but return to the nest a few hours later. Soon, however, they only come back to spend the night inside the nest box.

When several pairs are bred together, fledged young may enter the boxes or use the perches of strange breeding-pairs by mistake. Then it is possible that the intruders into the strange "territory" are chased off by the rightful owners, perhaps even bitten. De Grahl reports that some of his young birds sustained a bloody head as a result of such attacks.

Hybrids of the Nyasa have been bred as follows:

Nyasa Lovebird.

Africa, showing the range
of the Nyasa Lovebird.

Nyasa x Fischer's
Nyasa x Black-cheeked
Nyasa x Masked
Fischer's x Nyasa
Black-cheeked x Nyasa
Masked x Nyasa
Peach-faced x Nyasa

MUTATIONS

A Nyasa mutation, the Lutino, became known as early as in 1933. Prendergast in Adelaide, Australia, bred two Lutinos from two wild-colored birds. The parents are said to have been wild catches which were heterozygous for Lutino. A small strain of these

bright yellow birds with a red head and throat was successfully built up. In 1937, the first Lutino Nyasas came to Britain. In the U.S.A., Lutinos from wild-colored Nyasas were bred by Mrs. Reed (1940) and Mr. and Mrs. Rudkins (1951), all in California. Birds that were split for the Lutino factor therefore must have been in existence for some time unknown to anyone. Today it is unlikely that Lutino Nyasas are still found anywhere outside Australia and the U.S.A. Lutinos are described as fairly small, somewhat weak animals. It would seem that this mutation could not survive in the care of European breeders. For the inheritance, which is recessive, see Table 5.

A pair of Nyasa Lovebirds.

Fischer's Lovebird

Agapornis fischeri **Reichenow 1887**

DESCRIPTION

Length 15 cm. The forehead is bright orange, the rest of the head including the neck, throat, and upper breast is peach-colored to yellowish orange. The back of the head is more brownish, neck and upper breast more yellowish. Fischer's Lovebird is bright green above, yellowish green below. The upper tail-coverts are blue, likewise the tips of the green tail feathers. The outer tail feathers have yellowish borders and black bars near the tip, as well as a red-orange spot near the base. The eyes are brown, framed by broad, naked, white eye-rings. The strong bill is red, the narrow cere yellowish white. The feet are a pale bluish gray, the claws grayish brown. Male and female have the same coloration and are difficult to distinguish. In the hen the inner webs of the remiges are supposed to be black while being rather more gray in the cock. Other differentiating characteristics are size, shape of the head, color, and pelvic width. The female is slightly bigger, with a daintier head, less distinct colors in the head and breast regions, and during the breeding season a clearly palpable pelvic gap. In the male the pelvic bones are very close together, the head is bigger and more square. All these characteristics, however, vary considerably from one bird to another, making sexing very difficult, even for experienced aviculturists.

Juveniles have an altogether duller plumage, notably on the head. Depending on age, the bill, feet, and claws show striations or spots of varying degrees of darkness. At about three months the spots on the as yet pale red bill have disappeared, and at five months those on the feet also disappear. Nestlings are flesh-colored and covered in a red-orange down. At twelve days of age the eyes open, the bill, brownish at first, starts to redden, and the grayish green down begins to sprout.

RANGE AND BEHAVIOR

Fischer's Lovebird is found in northern Tanzania, particularly southeast of Lake Victoria. It has also become established near the town of Tanga on the Indian Ocean. Its natural habitat is the savannahs of the highlands at altitudes of 1000 to 1700 m. Particularly in regions which are more or less densely stocked with umbrella acacias and other trees, the Fischer's makes a regular appearance in small groups. In areas where corn and millet are grown, huge flocks frequently raid the fields. On such occasions a lot of noise is heard; these lovebirds make rather shrill whistling and screeching sounds. The birds prefer to look for their food on the ground but will feed directly off plants, shrubs, and trees as well. The diet includes both farinaceous and oily seeds, berries, and sweet fruit. Tender shoots and other green food are also taken.

Like the majority of lovebirds, Fischer's breed in a loose community of several pairs. As nesting sites they choose hollow trees, the deserted nests of the Rufous-tailed Weaver, hollows under the roofs of huts, and sometimes palm fronds as well. The nest is built with strips of bark, long, thin twigs, and leaf strips. It is a domed structure, fairly large, with an entrance hole on the side.

AVICULTURE

The bird was discovered by Dr. G. A. Fischer on his expedition from Pangani to Lake Victoria and named in his honor by Reichenow in 1887. In 1925, K. V. Painter of Cleveland, Ohio, received a single specimen. When, in 1927, more of these birds came to various European countries, the U.S.A., and Australia, successful breedings were soon accomplished everywhere. Since Fischer's was first imported, this bird has been the best-known and most popular of all the lovebirds.

It was easy to acclimate and breed and for this reason has survived the war and postwar years in Europe better than any of the other species. Today Fischer's are being bred successfully virtually everywhere. The birds marketed in this country will have been raised here too. They have been acclimated for generations and can, therefore, be kept in a garden aviary without any problems. They must, however, at all times have access to a frost-free room where they can shelter.

If desired, a pair of Fischer's may also be kept in a cage or small flight in an apartment. Here, too, the birds can be very interesting to watch. Their voices are not as loud and piercing as those of the Masked, let alone the Peach-faced Lovebirds. Kept indoors, the birds become fairly tame and give a lot of pleasure. To keep a single bird is also possible. If it is separated from its fellow Fischer's immediately after becoming independent and then kept on its own, it grows very attached to its keeper and becomes entirely hand-tame. With a lot of effort on the part of its owner the bird will even learn to talk to some extent. I would nevertheless advise against keeping a single bird, and once more refer the reader to my reasons for this in the introduction to this book.

BREEDING

Propagating Fischer's Lovebirds is not difficult if a good, healthy breeding pair is available. The greatest obstacle is the identification of the sexes. Anyone with little experience of these birds will find it virtually impossible to distinguish males and females.

When a well-matched pair has been found, they may be kept either in a cage or in a small separate aviary. It will not be long before the birds begin to mate.

The courtship behavior is very interesting. The partners run excitedly to and fro on a horizontal twig. The male flies around the female in small semicircles and lands beside her every so often. In between these flights he scratches himself on his head, reaching behind and around the wing. He makes soft sounds in rapid succession which resemble a clicking noise. Then the hen invites him to mate by spreading out and holding up her wings, cocking her tail, and laying her head back. The act of copulation, during which the male holds onto the hen's plumage with his claws, often lasts for one to two minutes. A nest box of the usual size must be hung up (two, in different locations, if the birds are kept in an aviary) and nesting material provided. The latter consists mainly of fresh twigs from willows, or from birches, fruit trees, and other broad-leaved trees, and of tough grasses.

The bark is chewed off the twigs and carried into the nest box in the bill. The hen is concerned with this task (only exceptionally has a male been seen to collect nesting material), and she also builds the large, domed nest. Every other day one egg is laid, and after the hen has produced the first or second egg she starts to incubate. The average number of eggs is four to six. Incubation takes twenty-one to twenty-three days. The newly hatched chicks are flesh-colored and covered with bright orange down. Their eyes are closed until the tenth or twelfth day. At about the same time the bill, brownish at first, shows a little red; the feet and claws, flesh-colored before, grow darker. Grayish green down appears and proper feathers begin to grow. After about thirty days the young are fully feathered. At thirty-five to thirty-seven days they fledge. The nestlings are fed by both parents, though after fledging predominantly by the father. About ten to fourteen days later they are independent.

Fischer's Lovebirds may also be bred in a larger aviary in colonies of several pairs. They are quite peaceable toward members of their own species, particularly when they have already been sharing an aviary for some time. What is important in such cases is to ensure that no single, unpaired bird is present in this colony. If there is, it can cause a lot of disturbance by trying to break up a pair and finding its own partner. A minimum of two nest boxes should be provided for each pair to prevent squabbling over the boxes. Where several pairs are kept together the breeding results are seldom as good as they are with separate pairs. Usually there is simply too much disturbance in a colony.

Fischer's Lovebirds.

Africa, showing the range
of the Fischer's Lovebird.

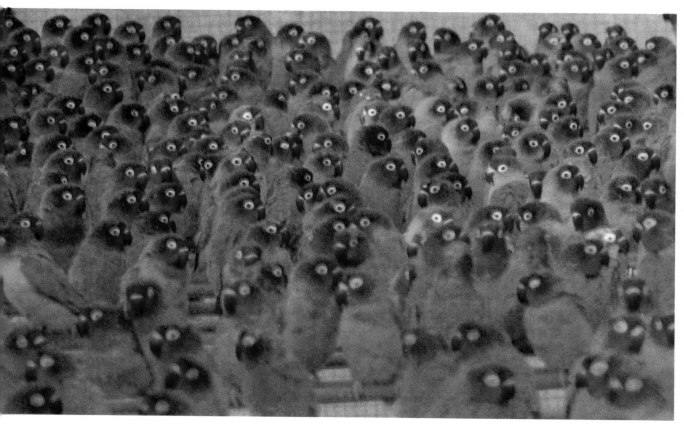

Recently imported Fischer's Lovebirds.

Hybrids have been produced with the following species:

Fischer's x Masked
Fischer's x Black-cheeked
Fischer's x Nyasa
Fischer's x Peach-faced
Masked x Fischer's
Black-cheeked x Fischer's
Nyasa x Fischer's
Peach-faced x Fischer's
Abyssinian x Fischer's

MUTATIONS

Yellow Fischer's Lovebirds appeared in the 1930s and were less rare in those days than they are today. Apparently, breeders in Japan and the U.S.A. are, however, in the process of building up new strains of this recessive mutation. For its inheritance, see Table 4.

Blue Fischer's were created in South Africa in 1957 and in California in the U.S.A. in 1959. To produce this mutation, a Blue Masked has to be crossed in. The first breeding stage is, therefore, as follows: (1) Blue Masked x Normal Fischer's (or vice versa). All the progeny from either of these pairings (*i.e.,* the F_1 generation) are heterozygous for Blue. To get this Blue factor into the Fischer's Lovebirds, the next pairing is as follows: (2) F_1 x Normal Fischer's (or vice versa). Of these young (the F_2 generation) 50% are heterozygous for Blue. As with the F_1 birds, these are impossible to distinguish from the wild-colored ones. It would, however, be wrong to mate a Blue Masked to an F_1 or F_2 bird. The correct pairing is (3) F_2 x F_2. This can result in the first Blue Fischer's, namely where two heterozygous birds come together. To increase the likelihood of this happening and to avoid the constant pairing of closely related birds, it is worthwhile to start off by breeding several pairs of Blue Masked x Normal Fischer's. The first Blue Fischer's can subsequently be mated according to Table 3, since this mutation is subject to recessive inheritance. The Blue Fischer's Lovebird shows the same beautiful blue color as its Masked counterpart, and the plumage of the head is white with a very slight touch of light gray.

Masked Lovebird

Agapornis personatus **Reichenow 1887**

DESCRIPTION

Length 14 to 16 cm. The whole head, the chin, and the upper part of the throat are black. The back of the head is more brown and changing to yellowish olive. A broad yellow band goes around the neck and breast. In older birds the breast can sometimes be orange rather than yellow. Remaining plumage bright green. Only the upper tail-coverts are pale blue. Tail feathers, from the tip, yellowish green on the upper sides. The narrow cere and the eye-rings are white, the eyes brown. The bill is bright red, the feet are bluish gray, the claws brown. The hen is of the same color as the cock, though usually bigger with a smaller, rounder head. The inner webs of the flight-feathers are said to be of a purer black in the hen, more grayish in the male. Juveniles are duller all over. There are black spots or striations on their feet and bill which fade at the age of about four months. In newly fledged young, the bill is still orange-colored to pale red with a bright red tip.

Nestlings are flesh-colored and have orange-red down above. The bill is light brown, the feet and claws are flesh-colored. At the age of ten days the egg-tooth drops off and the eyes start to open. By the time the chicks are twelve days old the second, grayish green down has already begun to sprout. At one month of age the young have their full plumage, and at thirty-five days they fledge.

RANGE AND BEHAVIOR

The Masked Lovebird comes from the interior of eastern Tanzania, where its range extends from Lake Manyara to Iringa. In the Dar Es Salaam area it was introduced by man, likewise in Nairobi and the Kenyan port of Mombasa where it flies about in mixed flocks with Fischer's Lovebirds and seems to interbreed with them as well. The habitat of the Masked is the grassy steppe at altitudes of 1,110 to 1,700 m, which is broken up only by an occasional grove of acacias and shrubs. There the Masked fly about in smallish groups or in flocks of over 100 birds, searching for food among the grasses, on the ground, and in the trees. They also fly to watering places in groups. In flight they constantly utter their loud, shrilly-piping, high-pitched calls. They fly quickly and in a straight line. The diet of the Masked consists of grass seeds, fruit, berries, leaf buds, blossoms, and an occasional insect. When the cereal crops are ripe, they love to invade the fields, especially where corn and millet are grown.

The nest is usually built in hollow trees, preferably baobab trees. It may, however, also be found under the roofs of huts and even in the nests of weavers and swifts. The hen gathers the nesting material—consisting mainly of strips of bark, shreds of palm fronds, twigs, and strong grass blades—and uses it to construct a large, domed nest.

AVICULTURE

The Masked Lovebird was discovered in 1877 by Dr. G. A. Fischer on his expedition and described in 1887 by Anton Reichenow. Another thirty-eight years elapsed, however, before the first import. The first Masked Lovebirds reached America in 1925 through the initiative of Mr. K. V. Painter. The latter was able to report the first successful breeding attempt in the spring of 1926 in Cleveland, Ohio. Europe saw the first consignment of these birds in 1927, and from 1928 onward they were imported in large quantities. Here, too, breeding success was quickly reported (according to *Gefiederte Welt,* 1928, the first breeders were Rambausek in Germany and Stager in Switzerland). In Britain and Australia Masked Lovebirds were propagated in the same year. Soon they were cultivated in many other countries as well.

The acclimation of newly imported birds was not easy. It had to be carried out in indoor birdrooms with a temperature of about 18 to 20°C. Outdoors the birds proved delicate at first, particularly in damp, cold weather. They soon got used to our climate, however. That they were fairly uncomplicated in other respects is indicated by the almost instant breeding successes. After they have been acclimated, the Masked can safely spend the winter in an indoor-outdoor connecting aviary. The indoor room need not be heated if the birds have access to a nest box at night. When the winter is spent in a warm house or a heated indoor aviary a nest box should not be provided; otherwise the birds might start to breed at the least favorable time of year. What is more, females still far too young would perhaps begin to lay.

Ideally, individual pairs should be kept in large cages. It is also possible to put a small flock of Masked Lovebirds into a spacious aviary. The birds will get on reasonably well. If such a colony includes an unpaired bird, however, the latter has difficulty in being accepted by the others and may get attacked by them. The Masked should not be associated with other species. These little parrots are simply too curious and aggressive. They usually bite other birds on the legs, which because of their strong beaks can result in severe injuries and even amputations.

Keeping a single bird is not recommended, as I have already pointed out with regard to the other lovebirds. Masked Lovebirds that have to be hand-reared or are separated from their parents and members of their own species at a very early age can become very affectionate and cute little pets, giving their owners a lot of pleasure. They are virtually unable to learn to talk, however; and their loud, shrill voices can become a nuisance.

BREEDING

As already mentioned, the Masked was bred in captivity for the very first time in 1926, in the U.S.A. Since then Masked Lovebirds have been cultivated regularly in large numbers. During and immediately after World War II their stocks, too, were severely decimated, but the Masked was the quickest of all lovebirds to make a complete recovery. Today they are still the most common species everywhere. The reason for this is simple: they are easy to breed.

As stated by Dr. M. Vriends in his book *Encyclopedia of Lovebirds,* as early as 1930 the Masked was bred in quantity in the U.S.A., in cages measuring 58 x 29 x 29 cm. The temporary ban on exports caused a setback to its husbandry, but these problems—usually caused by intense inbreeding—have long since been overcome. The Masked Lovebirds offered for sale today have almost exclusively been bred in captivity. They tend to be strong birds, entirely adapted to our climate. In frosty winter weather, however, they should remain indoors as their feet are prone to frostbite.

Breeding is likely to be most successful with one pair inside a spacious cage or small aviary. In the spring two nest boxes should be offered to the pair. Soon the mating drive begins to stir, the birds court, and the hen carries nesting material about with her in her bill. The courtship behavior is amusing to watch. The male trips around the female on the ground or, if she is perched on a branch, flies from one side to the other. Often the male scratches himself on the head (whereby he moves the foot around the wing and up to the head). Both partners trip excitedly to and fro on the branch. At last the hen invites the cock to mate by holding up her wings at an angle, lifting up her tail, and raising her head. As with all parrots, the act of copulation takes fairly long.

The main nesting material of the Masked is the bark of trees. The bark from willow twigs, birch, lindens, poplars, fruit trees and other

Masked Lovebird, normal coloration.

Africa, showing the range
of the Masked Lovebird.

The Blue mutation of the Masked Lovebird produces very beautiful birds. This mutation first occurred in the wild; its recessive inheritance is set out in Table 3.

developed, and at thirty-seven to forty days the young birds fledge. They continue to return to the nest box for a long while, however, spending the night there with their parents. After fledging, the young are fed predominantly by the male. Two weeks later they are fully independent.

Anyone who owns a very large outdoor aviary as well as several pairs of Masked which are already well used to one another might try to breed this species in a flock. This gives a great deal of satisfaction since it affords the opportunity to observe not only the behavior of individual pairs but also the social behavior that is displayed in a flock. The breeding result will, however, be more modest on the whole than it would be if each pair had been housed separately. The birds disturb each other too often for generally good results to be achieved. There may even be squabbles over nest boxes and nesting material. Broken eggs and young birds that have been thrown out of the nest are often the consequence when several pairs do not live together quite harmoniously.

broad-leaved trees is gnawed off in narrow strips and carried into one of the nest boxes by the hen. As the nest can be fairly large, the inner area of the box should measure 16 x 16 cm, with a height of 25 cm. The cock does not collect any nesting material, although he usually accompanies the hen on her flights to and from the box.

Four to six eggs are laid, as a rule—one every other day. The hen begins to incubate when the first egg has appeared so that the first chick hatches after about twenty-two days and another chick every other day thereafter. The nestlings are generally fed by both parents from the first day onward. Sometimes, however, the cock feeds only the hen to start with, and she then passes the food on to the young.

The chicks are flesh-colored, with red orange down above. At ten days their eyes open, and at about sixteen days their whole body is covered in grayish green fluff. Then the wings and tail feathers begin to sprout. After just five weeks the entire plumage is fully

At shows the best birds compete with one another. The winners have pretty rosettes affixed to their cages.

It is important that high humidity be maintained in the room or aviary; otherwise the chicks can get stuck inside the egg. The nest boxes can be sprayed with a plant sprayer at regular intervals. The regular provision of fresh nesting material should also be ensured. The hen throws dry bark out of the box and carries fresh bark back in. Often she will also take a bath and then sit on the eggs with wet plumage.

Hybrids of the Masked Lovebird have been bred with the following species:

Masked x Fischer's
Masked x Black-cheeked
Masked x Nyasa
Masked x Peach-faced
Masked x Abyssinian
Fischer's x Masked
Black-cheeked x Masked
Nyasa x Masked
Peach-faced x Masked
Abyssinian x Masked

MUTATIONS

The Blue mutation of the Masked developed in the wild. In 1927 Chapman (an animal dealer and collector) acquired a blue bird in Tanzania which he then sold to the Zoological Society of London. By the end of 1929, ten young split for Blue had been obtained from this bird. There were setbacks during the stabilization of the mutation. For example, one hen from the F_1 generation, split for Blue and mated to the Blue father, died of egg-binding. At the end of 1930, the pairing of two birds both split for Blue produced the first Blue Masked. Through Chapman, a few Tanzanian birds that were split for Blue though not known to be so were sent to France, and in 1935 M. Morin bred several blue specimens from this stock. He was able to build a stock of Blue Masked and to get it safely through the difficult war years. The U.S.A., too, seems to have received a few wild birds that were split for Blue, since Mr. Cross in California obtained the first Blue Masked Lovebirds ever bred in America when he mated a pair of normal birds.

Blue Masked were soon bred everywhere on a large scale. By 1950, Japan already exported them at a price similar to that of the wild color. To get as many Blue birds as possible, the breeders almost always mated Blue to Blue. Since the Blue factor is recessive, only this breeding method promised a 100% success rate. When pairing a bird split for Blue with a Blue, only 50% of the descendants will be Blue. The remaining 50% are again split for Blue, but these do not fetch the same high price as the homozygous Blue. Thus it was the breeders' own fault that the Blue individuals grew increasingly smaller and had less and less resistance to disease. In the 1960s, the Blue Masked once again became very rare and expensive in Europe. Today stocks have recovered, and the birds are big and strong, thanks to the responsible breeders who repeatedly paired big wild-colored birds to the Blue ones in order to strengthen the latter. While such pairings produce only heterozygous descendants, they are of the greatest importance for maintaining healthy stock. For the recessive inheritance of the Blue Masked, see Table 3.

Another mutation that has appeared is the Yellow Masked. These birds are not pure yellow (like the Golden Cherry Peach-faced, for example) but more or less washed with a little green. This means that some remnant of the blue structural color has been preserved in the feather cells. The inheritance of the Yellow mutation is recessive (see Table 4). The first Yellow Masked were cultivated by Mr. Scheu in Upland, California, in 1935. Later the mutation also appeared in Japan.

White Masked Lovebirds result when Blue is mated to Yellow (it is immaterial whether the Blue bird is the father or the mother). This variety was first produced in Japan in 1947. The birds concerned are not pure white but rather pale grayish-blue, with gray plumage on the head. Only the breast ring is almost pure white. The first birds of this variety came to Holland from Japan in 1955.

In Denmark a White Masked that possessed a mask of pure white was bred. Its parents were a Blue split for Yellow and a Green split for Yellow and Blue. For the inheritance of White, see Tables 6 and 10.

Inheritance Tables
for Color Varieties

In the tables below, two colors separated by a slash (*e.g.,* Green/Blue) means that the color in front of the slash is the dominant (*i.e.,* visible) one, whereas the color behind the slash is the recessive (*i.e.,* hidden) one. In the above example the Green bird is split for Blue. A bird may also be split for several colors—like the Green in Table 10 which is split for Blue, Yellow, and White. This is written: Green/Blue/Yellow/White.

Table 1: The dominant inheritance of the Pieds.

Since dominant inheritance precludes splits, there can be no birds which are split for Pied. Where two single-factor Pieds (Pieds I) are mated to each other, the progeny include double-factor Pieds (Pieds II). These two forms of Pied, which are of course impossible to distinguish externally, are inherited as follows:

(1) Pied I × Green = 25% Pieds I, 75% Greens
(2) Pied I × Pied I = 50% Pieds I, 25% Pieds II, 25% Greens
(3) Pied II × Green = 100% Pieds I
(4) Pied II × Pied I = 50% Pieds II, 50% Pieds I
(5) Pied II × Pied II = 100% Pieds II

Table 2: The intermediate inheritance of Dark-greens and Olive-greens.

The Dark-green and Olive-green colors are produced by combining Light-green (normal, or wild, color) with the dark factor. Because this dark factor is not a color but a character which determines the depth of a color shade, it could also be applied to other colors such as Light-blue. Then a single dark factor could be used to produce Cobalt-blue and a double dark factor to achieve Mauve birds.

(1) Light-green × Light-green = 100% Light-greens
(2) Light-green × Dark-green = 50% Light-greens, 50% Dark-greens
(3) Light-green × Olive-green = 100% Dark-greens
(4) Dark-green × Dark-green = 25% Light-greens, 50% Dark-greens, 25% Olive-greens
(5) Dark-green × Olive-green = 50% Dark-greens, 50% Olive-greens
(6) Olive-green × Olive-green = 100% Olive-greens

Table 3: The recessive inheritance of Blue.

(1) Blue × Blue = 100% Blues
(2) Blue × Green = 100% Greens/Blue
(3) Blue × Green/Blue = 50% Blues, 50% Greens/Blue
(4) Green/Blue × Green/Blue = 50% Greens/Blue, 25% Greens, 25% Blues
(5) Green/Blue × Green = 50% Greens, 50% Greens/Blue

Table 4: The recessive inheritance of Yellow, including Golden Cherry in the Peach-faced.

(1) Yellow × Yellow = 100% Yellows
(2) Yellow × Green = 100% Greens/Yellow
(3) Yellow × Green/Yellow = 50% Yellows, 50% Greens/Yellow
(4) Green/Yellow × Green/Yellow = 50% Greens/Yellow, 25% Greens, 25% Yellows
(5) Green/Yellow × Green = 50% Greens, 50% Greens/Yellow

Table 5: The recessive inheritance of Lutino.

(1) Lutino × Lutino = 100% Lutinos
(2) Lutino × Green = 100% Greens/Lutino
(3) Lutino × Green/Lutino = 50% Lutinos,
     50% Greens/Lutino
(4) Green/Lutino × Green/Lutino =
     50% Greens/Lutino, 25% Greens,
     25% Lutinos
(5) Green/Lutino × Green = 50% Greens,
     50% Greens/Lutino

Table 6: The recessive inheritance of White.

(1) White × White = 100% Whites
(2) White × Blue = 100% Blues/White
(3) White × Blue/White =
     50% Blues/White, 50% Whites
(4) Blue/White × Blue/White = 25% Blues,
     50% Blues/White, 25% Whites
(5) White × Green =
     100% Greens/Blue/Yellow/White
(6) Green/White × Green/White =
     6.25% Greens,
     12.50% Greens/Yellow,
     12.50% Greens/Blue,
     25.00% Greens/White,
     6.25% Yellows,
     12.50% Yellows/White
     6.25% Blues,
     12.50% Blues/White
     6.25% Whites

Lutino Peach-faced Lovebird.

Table 7: The sex-linked inheritance of Cinnamon.

(1) Cinnamon (Cock) × Cinnamon (Hen) =
     50% Cinnamons (Cocks),
     50% Cinnamons (Hens)
(2) Cinnamon (Cock) × Green (Hen) =
     50% Greens/Cinnamon (Cocks),
     50% Cinnamons (Hens)
(3) Green/Cinnamon (Cock) ×
     Cinnamon (Hen) =
     25% Greens/Cinnamon (Cocks),
     25% Cinnamons (Cocks),
     25% Greens (Hens),
     25% Cinnamons (Hens)
(4) Green (Cock) × Cinnamon (Hen) =
     50% Greens/Cinnamon (Cocks),
     50% Greens (Hens)
(5) Green/Cinnamon (Cock) ×
     Green (Hen) =
     25% Greens (Cocks),
     25% Greens/Cinnamon (Cocks),
     25% Greens (Hens),
     25% Cinnamons (Hens)

Table 8: The sex-linked inheritance of Lutino in the Peach-faced.

(1) Lutino (Cock) × Lutino (Hen) =
  50% Lutinos (Cocks),
  50% Lutinos (Hens)
(2) Lutino (Cock) × Green (Hen) =
  50% Greens/Lutino (Cocks),
  50% Lutinos (Hens)
(3) Green/Lutino (Cock) × Lutino (Hen) =
  25% Greens/Lutino (Cocks),
  25% Lutinos (Cocks),
  25% Greens (Hens),
  25% Lutinos (Hens)
(4) Green (Cock) × Lutino (Hen) =
  50% Greens/Lutino (Cocks),
  50% Greens (Hens)
(5) Green/Lutino (Cock) × Green (Hen) =
  25% Greens (Cocks),
  25% Greens/Lutino (Cocks),
  25% Greens (Hens),
  25% Lutinos (Hens)

American Yellow Peach-faced Lovebird.

Table 9: For the development of Albino Peach-faced Lovebirds.

The following pairings have been suggested by Dr. Erhard (*AZN* 8/75)

(1) Green/Blue/Lutino (Cock) × Blue (Hen) =
  12.50% Blues/Lutino (Cocks),
  12.50% Blues (Cocks),
  12.50% Greens/Blue/Lutino (Cocks),
  12.50% Greens/Blue (Cocks),
  12.50% Blues (Hens),
  12.50% Greens/Blue (Hens),
  12.50% Lutinos/Blue (Hens),
  12.50% Albinos (Hens)
(2) Green/Blue/Lutino (Cock) ×
  Lutino/Blue (Hen) =
  6.25% Blues/Lutino (Cocks),
  6.25% Greens/Lutino (Cocks),
  12.50% Greens/Blue/Lutino (Cocks),
  6.25% Lutinos (Cocks),
  12.50% Lutinos/Blue (Cocks),
  6.25% Albinos (Cocks),
  6.25% Blues (Hens),
  12.50% Greens/Blue (Hens),
  6.25% Greens (Hens),
  6.25% Lutinos (Hens),
  12.50% Lutinos/Blue (Hens),
  6.25% Albinos (Hens)

Table 10: The inheritance of the combinations Yellow × Blue and Green × White

(1) Yellow × Blue =
  100% Greens/Blue/Yellow/White
(2) Green × White =
  100% Greens/Blue/Yellow/White

Genetically these two combinations produce the same progeny. They are very useful birds which carry the factors for all four colors and, mated to each other, also produce offspring of all these colors.

(3) Green/Blue/Yellow/White ×
  Green/Blue/Yellow/White =
  6.25% Greens,
  12.50% Greens/Blue,
  12.50% Greens/Yellow,
  25.00% Greens/White,
  6.25% Blues,
  12.50% Blues/White,
  6.25% Yellows,
  12.50% Yellows/White,
  6.25% Whites

DISEASES OF PARROTS

Preface

It is only during the last fifteen years that diseases of fowl as a special field has become an established component of research and teaching at the veterinary institutes. The purpose and goal of the newly established professorial chairs have been to provide preventive and curative veterinary services to the economically important poultry industry.

For some time these institutes or clinics have also been consulted by the owners of ornamental birds, since the majority of practicing veterinarians are not always familiar with the problems of bird diseases. Because of the tremendous difference from the treatment of fowl bred on a massive scale for human consumption—where the individual animal is of no consequence but the health of the herd as a whole must rank as the top priority—special bird clinics have been set up. I am deeply indebted to my respected and admired teacher, Prof. Dr. Otfried Siegmann, director of the Clinic for Fowl at the Veterinary Institute of Hanover, for giving me the opportunity to supervise the Clinic for Ornamental and Wild Birds from 1974 to 1979. The knowledge gained there, broadened by work in my own practice, forms the basis for the subsequent chapters on psittacine diseases in this book.

Considering that only a few people are working in the field of bird diseases—and only began doing so relatively recently—the body of knowledge in this special branch of veterinary science is bound to be full of gaps. Continuing close cooperation between experienced aviculturists and practicing veterinarians remains absolutely essential.

The list of diseases that follows in no way aspires to completeness. My aim is, instead, to select those clinical pictures which the layman may learn to identify or which can be observed fairly frequently. On no account are the suggestions for treatment intended to encourage do-it-yourself therapy! Consultation with an experienced veterinarian is absolutely vital in every case.

The following has fulfilled its purpose if the bird owner is stimulated into thinking and doing something about the diseases of his pets and gains a growing awareness of his responsibility for the well-being of the living creatures in his care.

Dr. Manfred Heidenreich
Hanover, Fall 1980

Note: Generic names of some of the proprietary drugs mentioned in the text can be found under the trade-name entry in the Index.

Parasitic Diseases

MANGE IN BUDGERIGARS

Synonym: Scaly Face.

Cause: A mange mite *(Knemidocoptes pilae)* parasitizing in or under the skin.

Incidence: This mite occurs almost exclusively in Budgerigars, although there have been exceptional cases when it was isolated from Cockatiels and lovebirds. These parasites are of great significance in Budgerigar flocks and are transmitted from bird to bird by direct contact. Depending on the host's resistance, visible pathologic changes may sometimes not appear until up to six months have elapsed.

Clinical picture: Mainly on the unfeathered areas of the external skin grayish white, crusty-porous deposits can be observed. These generally first appear at the angle of the beak and may subsequently spread over the whole beak, the eyelids, legs, and cloaca. Due to burrows in the region of the cere, infestation with mange-mites frequently results in deformities of the beak. In the early stages of the disease the birds suffer from itchiness and scratch themselves a great deal. As the illness progresses, however, itchiness can usually no longer be observed.

Diagnosis: Isolation of the causal agent from a skin scraping after dissolving the horny deposits with caustic lye. The signs are, however, so characteristic that a diagnosis can be made simply by looking at the patient.

Prevention and treatment: Treatment of an infected population is bound to be difficult since each bird requires intensive individual treatment. Example: Paint beak, eyelids, legs, and cloaca (even if only one part of the body appears to have been affected) with a suspension of one part water and one part Odylen.® This therapy *must* be given three times at five-day intervals. In particularly severe cases a fourth treatment may be added. If this is followed by isolation, there is no possibility of a relapse. Reinfections are, however, possible at all times.

ECTOPARASITES

Cause: Feather lice *(Mallophagen),* feather-quill mites, red mites.

Incidence: Whereas lice and feather-quill mites permanently parasitize the bird, red mites attack their hosts only by night while spending the day in cracks and crevices in the birds' surroundings. Lice and feather-quill mites are transmitted by direct contact; the red mite migrates and therefore feeds on the blood of several birds.

Clinical picture: (1) Feather lice: Living as they do mainly on feather material and dead skin, infestation with these parasites represents no danger to life. The constant itchiness however can undermine the well-being of affected birds. An external sign of the infestation is partially consumed feathers. (2) Feather-quill mites: These mites parasitize subcutaneously in the localities of feather formation (feather papillae) and during feather growth penetrate into the blood-filled shaft of the developing feather. Characteristic are the following feather abnormalities: as soon as the feather has grown to half its size, the blood supply suddenly dries up (giving the shaft a certain resemblance to an hour-glass) and eventually the shaft breaks off at this site. Infestation is usually confined to the large feathers. (3) Red mite: The red mite sucks the host's blood, and the resultant blood loss can cause serious damage, particularly in nestlings. Because of the blood loss, affected birds have a gray, wrinkled skin and look debilitated and apathetic.

Diagnosis: (1) Feather lice: They are readily identified, among the contour feathers and on the underside of the wing, as tiny, elongated moving objects. (2) Feather-quill mites: These can be isolated only upon the removal of a blood feather. Since the parasites migrate as soon as the quill has cooled off, it is essential that the diagnostic material be securely packed (*e.g.,* by heat-sealing it into plastic foil). For

A Budgerigar suffering from mange-mite infestation of moderate severity. The gray porous deposits on the cere and in the angle of the beak are clearly visible. As a direct consequence of the infestation, affected birds frequently develop malformations of the beak since the burrowing activities of the parasites injure the growth zone.

the examination the feather material is dissolved so that the parasites become visible. (3) Red mite: Usually found when the potential hiding-places are investigated. Where a single bird is kept, a white cloth can be folded to cover the cage at night and then examined the following morning.

Prevention and treatment: (1) Feather lice: All birds—the entire stock—should be sprinkled twice with powder (*e.g.,* Alguan®) with a ten-day interval between treatments. (2) Feather-quill mite: No treatment known. (3) Red mite: Application of contact insecticides with a carbaryl base, preferably in aerosol form.

Close up of bird louse on a feather. The glassy eggs of this parasite can be seen on the right.

Feather lice (*Mallophagen*) on the underside of the wing.

THREADWORMS

Cause: Various *Capillaria* species.

Transmission: Whereas some threadworms occurring in other bird species need intermediate hosts (*e.g.,* earthworms) for their developmental cycle, the species observed in parrots undergo a direct development. Inside the egg, which is expelled with the droppings, an infectious larval stage develops which, after ingestion of this egg by a new host, affects the mucosa of the digestive system.

Clinical picture: Although mortality among parrots due to threadworm infestation is rare, every such case is important in that it lowers the resistance of the host. The most frequent organ attacked by threadworms is the small intestine of the birds, leading to diarrhea with subsequent emaciation. In some cases the threadworms may also colonize the mucous membrane of the buccal cavity and crop, which can result in yellowish crusty deposits reminiscent of trichomoniasis. Birds affected in this way have difficulty swallowing.

Postmortem: Depending on the affected area, the mucous membrane involved may show signs of severe inflammation.

Diagnosis: Isolation of threadworm eggs from the bird's feces by means of flotation.

Prevention and treatment: As with roundworms, preventive measures consist of cleaning, disinfection, and maximal hygiene. Since threadworms do not enjoy a long life span, the host has a chance of ridding itself of them without intervention if reinfections can be prevented. In the past, treatment for threadworm infestation presented some difficulties because the medicines used were not well tolerated. Today, however, preparations are available which directly affect the parasite inside the host. Example: as in the treatment for roundworms, Concurat-L® or Panacur® at a dosage of 15 mg/kg body weight on two successive days.

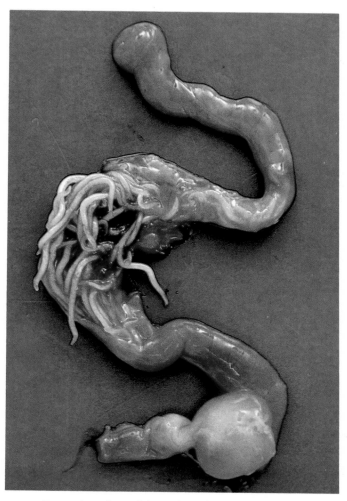

Stomach and small intestine of a parakeet. The small intestine is entirely filled with roundworms. Abrupt treatment in this case would mean certain death since the intestine would get blocked by the tangled mass of dead worms. Where an infestation of this severity is suspected, treatment during the first few days should consist of very small doses of an anthelminthic to kill off the worms gradually, in small numbers.

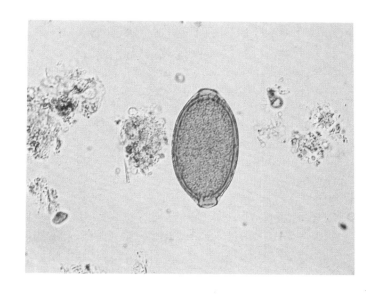

A threadworm egg as seen through the microscope during a parasitological examination of feces. Characteristic are the two polar caps of the egg, which give it a lemon-like appearance.

TAPEWORMS

Cause: Various tapeworm species, which in many exotic birds have not yet been identified. Most of them, however, are flat, segmented, and whitish in appearance and can be recognized by the layman.

Incidence and transmission: Tapeworms occur predominantly in the larger parrots and may parasitize these for many years without being noticed. For their development these parasites, which live in the small intestine, require an intermediate host (*e.g.,* snails, worms, or insects), which are then ingested by the final host. Since such intermediate hosts do not exist in our latitudes, a reinfection of exotic birds is not possible.

Clinical picture: Affected birds only rarely show any signs of disease. Debility, emaciation, and diarrhea are observed in severe cases of infestation.

Postmortem: The small intestine contains mature tapeworms, usually without any pathological changes of the intestinal mucosa.

Diagnosis: The diagnosis is based on the presence of shed tapeworm segments (*proglottids)* in the feces. Their detection is possible only with the aid of a microscope. It can happen however, that longer segments of a tapeworm protrude from the cloaca and the diagnosis is thus made easy.

Treatment: A single dose of, for instance, Mansonil® (200 mg/kg body weight) or Droncit® . Both preparations are well tolerated.

ROUNDWORMS

Cause: Various species of ascarids.

Transmission: These parasites do not need an intermediate host but are picked up directly. The excreted eggs are extremely resistant in the outside environment and survive for a long period. To mature, the eggs require moisture and warmth. Ingestion occurs via contaminated food and water as well as infected earthworms which themselves have swallowed feces containing eggs. The earthworm, being a carrier, can be a reservoir for many infectious roundworm eggs.

Clinical picture: In parakeets severe infestation with roundworms remains the most frequent cause of mortality. Infected birds suffer excessive weight loss, have rough-looking plumage, and usually present with runny, liquid feces. The disease may continue over many weeks until the bird finally dies. As a result of the toxins produced by these worms, there may be paralysis of the legs and wings. Severely infested birds may be seen to vomit owing to blockage of the intestinal passage by tangled masses of worms.

Postmortem: Quite often a high degree of blockage of the small intestine will be observed, with over a hundred parasites. Roundworms being relatively large (about 5 cm), the whole intestine may be filled with them in some cases. Inflammations of the mucosa are noted as well.

Diagnosis: Isolation of roundworm eggs from the excrement of the birds by means of flotation.

Prevention and treatment: Prevention includes scrupulous cleanliness, disinfection, and examination of fecal specimens at regular intervals. Earthworms must be kept at bay! If all else fails, the aviaries may have to be protected with tiles or concrete. Drugs which have proved effective are levamisole, mebendazole, and febendazole.

Example: Concurat-L® , 7.5 gm per three liters of water over four days. Repeat twenty-one days later.

COCCIDIOSIS

Cause: Unicellular parasites which primarily invade the intestinal mucosa.

Transmission: Within the intestinal mucosa the parasites produce oocysts, which are excreted in the feces. Because of their thick shell they are extremely able to cope with environmental conditions. Under optimal conditions oocysts need at least two days in the external environment in order to themselves become infective. After ingestion by a new host the sporocysts which have since formed are liberated from the oocysts. The sporocysts develop into sporozoites which attack the intestinal cells. Since these stages are capable of repeated asexual reproduction as well, one oocyst that has been ingested can be responsible for infecting many hundreds of intestinal cells. After only four to seven days from the initial infection the new host can already excrete oocysts himself.

Clinical picture: Coccidia use up vitamin B, hence all symptoms of vitamin-B deficiency (*q.v.*) may be observed. The most damaging effect lies in the destruction of the intestinal mucosa. This results in bleeding from the intestine, and in severe cases the intestine can become very red and swollen and may be visible through the thin skin of the abdomen. Additional signs are weight loss and diarrhea (with the presence of undigested seeds in the feces). In older birds the disease is rarely very marked. Affected juveniles, however, shortly after fledging and thus feeding independently for the first time, generally show a range of clearer clinical signs, which may terminate fatally.

Postmortem: Depending on severity, the intestinal contents will be bloody or slimy. Inflammation of the intestinal mucosa.

Diagnosis: Isolation of excreted oocysts from the feces by a special method of flotation, and examination under the microscope.

Prevention and treatment: Prevention must aim at keeping the degree of infection as low as possible. Frequent cleaning, disinfection, and fecal examination help achieve this. Drugs that have proved effective are sulphonamides and amprolium. Examples: first three days: amprolium added to the drinking water; fourth and fifth day: vitamins A and D$_3$; sixth to eighth day: as per first three days; ninth to eleventh day: a multivitamin preparation.

TRICHOMONIASIS

Cause: Trichomonas gallinae, a unicellular, pear-shaped parasite of mucous membranes, with four paired flagella anteriorly, an undulating membrane, and an axostyle.

Incidence and transmission: The causal agent undoubtedly has the greatest significance for pigeons, although it is also found in parrots and birds of prey. Mature birds usually carry a latent (hidden) infection without the appearance of any pathological signs. Juveniles from time to time become infected via the contents of the parents' crop, where injuries to the mucous membranes through seeds encourage the onset of the infection.

Clinical picture: Affected birds characteristically show a yellowish crusty deposit in the region of the buccal cavity and crop ("buccal-cavity–crop form"). The birds present with weakness, crop deposits, a reduced food intake, and diarrhea. In nestlings, inflammatory changes of the umbilicus can appear as well. In rare cases, internal organs such as the liver and heart may also be affected ("generalized form").

Postmortem: Yellowish crusty deposits in buccal cavity, esophagus, and crop. In some cases there are also deposits on the liver, heart, lungs, and air sacs.

Diagnosis: Where the changes are severe it will be possible to make a provisional diagnosis simply by noting the clinical signs. It is, however, necessary to confirm the diagnosis by isolating the causal agent from a mucous specimen taken from the buccal cavity and crop. The mucus is examined under a phase-contrast microscope.

Prevention and treatment: It is most important to break the chain of infection by treating adult birds that carry the causal agent, thus preventing them from transmitting the disease. Additionally, disinfecting the drinking water has proved advantageous. One drug which has shown itself to be highly effective, both in prophylaxis and therapy, is carnidazole (Spartrix®). A single dose of one tablet per 500 gm body weight should be given. The deposits on the mucous membranes must on no account be removed by mechanical means since this would result in severe hemorrhages. Where the changes are very marked the discomfort may be eased somewhat by painting on a solution of iodized glycerin.

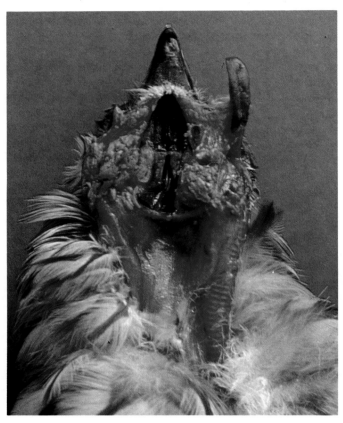

The buccal cavity (opened from below) of a bird that died of trichomoniasis. The changes resemble those caused by a fungal infection. The deposits are, however, so firmly anchored to the mucosa that severe hemorrhages would result if they were removed. Such manipulations should be avoided. The usual cause of death in a case of trichomonal infection is the inability to swallow food or a displacement of the trachea due to deposits.

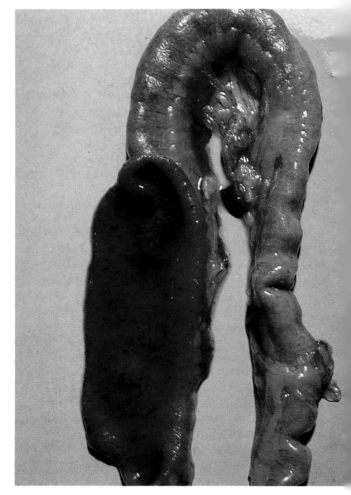

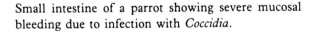

Small intestine of a parrot showing severe mucosal bleeding due to infection with *Coccidia*.

Bacterial and Viral Diseases

INFLAMMATION OF THE CROP MUCOSA

Cause: Infections with bacteria or fungi, corrosion, poisoning, constipation, processes of fermentation inside the crop.

Incidence: Common in Budgerigars and parrots after ingestion of food or water contaminated with feces. Mucosal infections with fungi and trichomonads (which also occur in healthy birds) followed by lowered resistance can lead to inflammation. The disease is rarely transmitted to other occupants of the cage, however, except where a pair of birds is involved and mutual feeding may result in transmission of the causal agent.

Clinical picture: An inflammation of the crop mucosa expresses itself in reduced food intake, apathy, and fluffing of the feathers. The nutritional condition gradually worsens.

With pumping movements of the neck, the patients often vomit up seeds and a viscous, stringy, grayish white slime. Due to head-shaking the plumage of the head is severely matted ("head-sweating"). Without treatment the birds often die.

Postmortem: Depending on the cause, slimy grayish white deposits on the crop mucosa; at least, however, severe redness and swelling.

Diagnosis: Because the disease runs a relatively characteristic course, a provisional diagnosis is easily made. The primary cause is often difficult to establish, however. X-rays with contrast media are valuable diagnostic aids. Where microorganisms are involved and treatment is continued over a long period, isolation of the causal agent by means of a sensitivity test should be undertaken.

A Budgerigar with severely matted plumage of the head resulting from an inflammation of the crop mucosa. Laymen refer to this phenomenon as "head sweating."

Treatment: In my own experience two injections with a broad-spectrum antibiotic, with cortisone and vitamin A at two-day intervals, have proved quite effective. In addition, the crop should be rinsed thoroughly and an antibiotic applied locally as well. The administration of an antibiotic via the drinking water (*e.g.,* Terramycin-Hen® , 10 gm per liter of water) over a period of five days also makes good sense.

SALMONELLOSIS

Cause: A bacterium, most commonly *Salmonella typhimurium.*

Transmission: The most frequent sources of infection are water and food which have been contaminated with *Salmonella,* notably foods with a high protein content such as fish and meats, shrimps, and bone meal. The bacteria also multiply on the surface of the water (infrequently cleaned drinking vessels). A particularly important role in their transmission is played by wild birds found near, or even on top of, the aviaries. In the same way the presence of rats and mice also gives cause for concern.

Clinical picture: The signs of this disease are relatively uncharacteristic. Weakness, sitting with fluffed feathers, and diarrhea are often the only obvious abnormalities. Usually, however, several birds among the stock are affected, which indicates the infectious character of the condition. Surviving birds may excrete the pathogens for the rest of their lives!

Postmortem: In the majority of cases there is severe distension of the major organs, such as liver, spleen, and kidneys. In addition, these organs often show extremely fine yellow speckles (necrotic foci). A further sign, which is almost always observed, is an inflammation of the intestinal mucosa (which varies in severity).

Diagnosis: The causal agent can be isolated from fecal specimens—however, special bacteriological methods are necessary for this. Since the pathogens are not excreted constantly, only repeated testing at intervals of several days is conclusive.

Prevention and treatment: Birds that have been newly purchased should be put into special quarantine cages by their owner while the necessary fecal examinations are carried out. On no account must they be allowed to join the existing stock until it is certain that they are free from *Salmonella.* A number of broad-spectrum antibiotics are suitable for the treatment of salmonellosis. However, since the pathogens have the distinction of being unusually resistant to these drugs, it is advisable to request a sensitivity test. In this way all but the most effective agent can be eliminated. So far, chloramphenicol (*caution:* feather abnormalities are a possible side-effect) and a combination of sulphonamides and trimethoprim have produced the best results.

E. COLI INFECTION

Cause: Various strains of the bacterium *Escherichia coli.*

Transmission: E. coli form part of the normal intestinal flora in a great many species of birds without giving rise to morbid symptoms. But in seed-or fruit- eaters these germs do not belong to the normal flora of the gut; in these species they must consequently be regarded as potential pathogens. The most common sources of infection are food and water which have been contaminated with droppings.

Clinical picture: The signs of the disease are uncharacteristic as a rule, apart from the fact that nearly all affected birds are observed to suffer from diarrhea. Particularly susceptible are juveniles and weakened older birds. Frequently, therefore, it is necessary for several factors to be present before the disease is triggered.

Postmortem: Like the course of the disease, dissection also fails to present a uniform picture. Apart from inflammatory changes of the intestinal mucosa, the major organs, such as liver, spleen, and kidney, are sometimes found to be distended.

Diagnosis: A diagnosis of this disease is possible only with bacteriological examination of the feces or internal organs. However, since the presence of *E. coli* in the feces does not necessarily mean these bacteria are in fact acting as pathogens, their isolation from the organs (preferably from birds that have just died) is more conclusive.

Prevention and treatment: Particularly where this disease is concerned, it is of the utmost importance to ensure that high standards of hygiene are being maintained throughout. This applies above all to the quality of food and water. The birds should not be allowed to come in contact with their excreta. A number of broad-spectrum antibiotics are available for use in treatment. Unfortunately, however, various strains of *E. coli* have become highly resistant to some of these. If therapy is to be effective, therefore, it needs to be preceded by sensitivity tests.

TUBERCULOSIS

Cause: A bacterium, most commonly *Mycobacterium avium;* in rare cases, *Mycobacterium tuberculosis,* the agent of human tuberculosis, is the cause.

Incidence and transmission: Avian tuberculosis is one of the most common causes of mortality among birds in zoological gardens. The pathogens, which can survive for years in the external environment, are usually picked up with the food, although infections may also result from the inhalation of airborne bacteria. Transmission from bird to man and vice versa is possible.

Clinical picture: Tuberculosis, an insidious disease characterized by progressive weight loss, often continues for months. Until shortly before their death, affected birds show few if any distinct abnormalities. In some cases large tubercles may form in internal organs, which can lead to lameness of the limbs. In tuberculosis of the lungs and air sacs the patients present with respiratory disturbances. Where the digestive apparatus is involved (the most common form of the disease) diarrhea can be observed. Other forms of the disease that occur are tuberculosis of the skeleton and various types affecting the skin.

Postmortem: Depending on the locality, pinhead- to walnut-sized fatty nodules are found in the organs. Often these nodules can be felt even through the outer layer of the skin.

Diagnosis: Unfortunately the tuberculin test, conclusive in other animals, is not very reliable in birds. In the same way, an analysis of the blood may not be useful. A provisional diagnosis however can be made by looking at the patient's general condition in conjunction with an X-ray (although the latter will show only the larger nodules).

Prevention and treatment: Because of the prolonged course of this disease, preventive measures are very difficult if not impossible to implement. Treatment, too, is almost always unsuccessful and, because the disease can be transmitted to humans, should not be attempted at all. It is important that the bodies of tuberculous animals be effectively destroyed!

PSITTACOSIS

Incidence and transmission: Psittacosis is a disease of parrots and Budgerigars which is transmissible to humans, in whom it can cause severe symptoms and, if it is not recognized in time, even death. There is little doubt that imported birds and nonadherence to the strict legal requirements (quarantine) are of significance in the transmission of the disease. Psittacosis can be spread by droplet infection, through dirt and smear infections, and other living and nonliving factors.

Clinical picture: There is no characteristic main symptom. Sleepiness, loss of appetite, and weight loss are general symptoms. In addition, one may observe not only diarrhea but also rhinitis and conjunctivitis. The duration of the disease can be anywhere from just a few days to three to four weeks. Amazons and African Grey Parrots appear to be particularly susceptible. Where newly purchased birds of these species show the symptoms just described, psittacosis (a reportable disease) should be suspected. Although the disease is highly infectious, it can happen that only a few birds among the stock actually contract it. Those that have recovered from the infection may excrete the causal agents for the rest of their lives.

Postmortem: While a tentative diagnosis on a living bird is difficult to make, dissected material tends to provide clues much more readily. Severe swelling of liver and spleen, inflammations of the intestine, and inflammatory changes of the respiratory tract (notably the air sacs) are indicative of psittacosis.

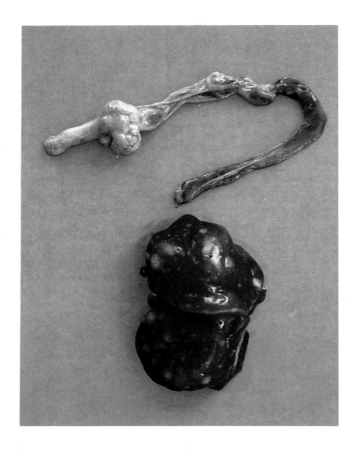

Above: Tuberculosis lesions in the liver and rectum of a parrot. A bird suffering from tuberculosis of the liver and intestine will have been excreting the pathogens in the feces and infecting the aviary for a long while.

Below: Skin changes around the bases of the beak caused by Agapornid pox virus.

Diagnosis: This is based on postmortem results plus isolation of the causal agent. The latter task is difficult and time-consuming since living laboratory mice have to be used for the cultivation of these microorganisms. Often it takes as long as three to four weeks for results to become available. Suitable sources for specimens are the liver, spleen, and kidney as well as excreta.

Prevention and treatment: [In Germany] in addition to scrupulous adherence to official regulations, every newly acquired bird should be subjected to private quarantine. Where an infection is present the stock may be treated only by a designated veterinary officer. As required by law, treatment must extend over a period of thirty days for Budgerigars and forty-five days for other species.

AVIAN POX

Cause: A pox virus specific to lovebirds.

Incidence and transmission: Specific pox viruses have so far been isolated from chickens, pigeons, turkeys, quail, canaries, and lovebirds. The causal agents are transmitted by direct contact, by insects that pierce the skin to suck blood, or by skin parasites.

Clinical picture: There are two different courses the disease may take: the first, the "mucosal form," is characterized by the presence of yellowish crusty deposits in the oral cavity and is not unlike trichomoniasis in its clinical picture. The second, the "skin form," is more common. Here one observes pinhead- to pea-sized skin pox, notably in the angle of the beak, on the eyelids, and in the unfeathered areas of the external skin. Where the skin is affected the disease tends to run a fairly benign course, with the changes clearing up spontaneously after a few weeks. The mucosal form, on the other hand, may result in mortalities.

Postmortem: Usually nothing abnormal is detected where the internal organs are concerned.

Diagnosis: Isolation of causal agent by means of hen's egg culture or cytological examination of pox material.

Prevention and treatment: Preventive measures are possible with all susceptible species except lovebirds, for which no vaccines have so far become available. Since birds suffering from viral diseases are particularly prone to additional infections, treatment should be confined to preventing secondary conditions. Broad-spectrum antibiotics may be administered for this purpose. In addition, local treatment by painting iodized glycerin on the skin in the affected areas can sometimes bring relief. It is important that sick birds have a high vitamin intake. Wherever possible, biting or blood-sucking insects and other vectors of disease must be kept at bay.

NEWCASTLE DISEASE

Cause: A virus which occurs in a great many avian species and is of special significance in fowl.

Transmission: The virus first appeared in Southeast Asia and was subsequently carried to Europe by parrots. From there it spread to all parts of the world. At collection points in the exporting countries juvenile parrots are still all too often kept in association with fowl so that transmission of the disease is possible. Subsequent shipment and quarantine may then result in mass mortalities. The disease can also be transmitted by humans, as well as tools and equipment.

Clinical picture: Nearly all affected birds die within the relatively short period of six to nine days from the onset of the disease. Diarrhea, discharge from nostrils and eyes, involuntary movements, paralysis, torticollis, and dyspnea are observed. Because the disease is highly infectious, virtually the entire stock perishes within a short time.

Postmortem: As would be expected in view of the acute course of the disease, no serious organic changes can be observed. Most organs merely show hemorrhages of varying severity. Fine hemorrhages in the mucosa of the proventriculus are sometimes characteristic. Cerebral hemorrhages are also observed.

Diagnosis: An outbreak of Newcastle disease always reaches epidemic proportions, wiping out the great majority of the affected bird population. The disease is of short duration, lasting just a few days. A final diagnosis is only possible by means of isolating the virus from the organs of dead birds.

Prevention and treatment: Because this disease is extremely dangerous, particularly to the poultry industry, it is reportable, and all countermeasures must be initiated by the designated veterinary officer. Since treatment is ineffective, it is important to aim at prevention. Vaccination with the available vaccines intended for poultry may prevent the disease if a slightly higher dose is given. Since for large parrots the risk of infection is greatest in their country of origin, they should be vaccinated there.

Fungal Infections

CANDIDIASIS, MONILIASIS

Cause: Various species of yeast fungi, particularly *Candida albicans.*

Incidence: The causal agent is present on the mucous membranes of healthy animals and causes diseases only when resistance is lowered.

Clinical picture: These fungi cause changes of the mucous membranes in the region of the upper digestive tract, *i.e.,* the buccal cavity, the esophagus, and especially the crop. Diseases of the crop caused by these organisms are no rarity in parrots. The birds present with yellowish cheesy, sometimes smeary, deposits which—unlike those seen in trichomoniasis—can readily be wiped off without resultant hemorrhages.

In an advanced stage the crop mucosa appears thickened, the bird clearly eats less, and then vomits up grayish white, very stringy slime which, due to head-shaking, ends up on the plumage of the head. Uncontrolled, prolonged administration of antibiotics and a deficiency of vitamin A can predispose birds to this disease.

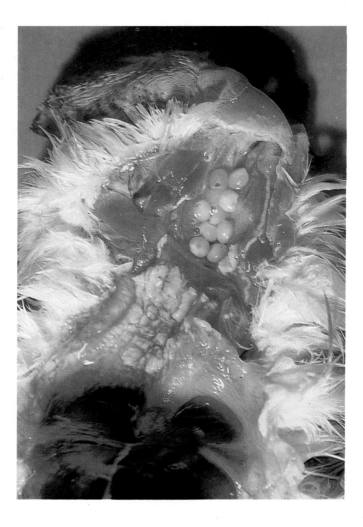

Above: The dissected esophagus and crop of a Budgerigar. The crop mucosa shows grayish yellow deposits caused by a fungal infection, *Candida albicans*. Below: Foot and lower thigh of a lovebird suffering from a fungal infection of the skin.

Postmortem: Deposits (easily mistaken for those seen in trichomoniasis) in the buccal cavity, esophagus, crop, and proventriculus.

Diagnosis: The disease can be identified only by determining the presence of the causal agent by swabbing the affected mucous membrane. The presence of the fungus can be determined microscopically by means of a culture.

Prevention and treatment: For the prevention of the disease, an adequate intake of vitamin A is required. Caution, however: excessive doses of this vitamin can be harmful. Treatment should be carried out with the drug Moronal® . Good results have been achieved with a dosage of 0.2 gm per liter of drinking water over a period of seven days. Additional topical treatments with iodized glycerin is useful.

FUNGAL DISEASES OF THE SKIN

Cause: Various skin fungi, *e.g., Trichophyton* species.

Incidence and transmission: Infection is usually the result of direct contact from bird to bird, which means that breeding pairs or young birds from the same clutch are frequently affected together.

Clinical picture: Particularly in Amazons, Cockatiels and cockatoos, brownish smeary deposits, which can cause severe itching and irritation, are observed in the affected areas (from the inside of the thighs toward the rump). Persistent pecking in the affected areas quickly makes them larger. Parallel with this, loss of feathers occurs.

Postmortem: The only visible abnormalities are the skin changes already mentioned.

Diagnosis: Despite the typical localization, it is important to isolate the causal agent in all cases.

Treatment: Quite effective broad-spectrum antifungal preparations are Canesten® and Pimafucin® . Both are available in aqueous solution or in ointment form and should be applied to the affected areas of the skin two or three times a day for over a minimum period of fourteen days. The outer edges of the lesions should be treated particularly intensively since the fungus spreads outward in rings.

ASPERGILLOSIS

Cause: Various *Aspergillus* (mold fungus) species, most commonly *Aspergillus fumigatus* and *Aspergillus niger.*

Incidence and transmission: Molds are common everywhere in the external environment. The spores (resting stages) are highly resistant and under favorable conditions can cause fungal infection. Warmth and dampness promote the growth of molds. Particularly susceptible are young birds, especially the nestlings of birds that breed in cavities. Thus the bedding inside the nest box is of great hygienic significance. Peat, hay, and straw are unsuitable; however, wood shavings from conifers (untreated) are appropriate because the resins prevent fungal growth. Most frequently the causal agents are inhaled, which means the respiratory system becomes infected.

Clinical picture: Unfortunately this infection tends to go unnoticed until visible or audible respiratory disturbances have set in. The birds gasp for breath. In advanced cases the trachea already shows tall fungal "meadows." Juveniles and older birds die despite treatment if presented at this late stage. Aspergillosis is, however, a disease which mostly affects birds whose resistance has already been weakened through adverse feeding or housing conditions or other diseases.

Postmortem: Dissection of birds that have died of the disease shows a fairly characteristic picture. In the lung numerous yellowish foci the size of a pinhead can be seen. Inside the air sacs deposits are found, some of them quite extensive, which may be crusty with a greenish, powdery surface. The growths inside these hollow organs remind one of moldy bread.

Diagnosis: On the living bird a diagnosis is difficult, if not impossible. Examinations of blood serum have not proved helpful. In conjunction with the preliminary report, an X-ray may be of use, although only advanced changes will show. Diagnosis on a dead bird is made by isolating the causal agents from the affected organs.

Prevention and treatment: In the early stages treatment with the drug Daktar® may

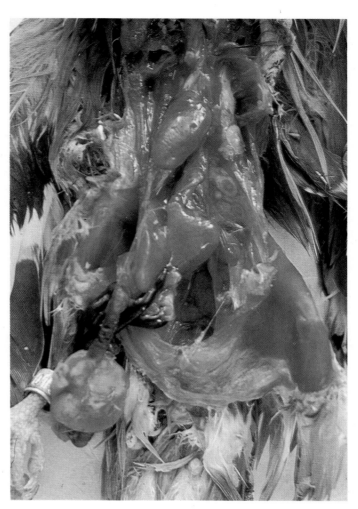

Section of a Budgerigar with aspergillosis in the air sacs and lung. At this stage the lesions still have circular boundaries. At an advanced stage the air sacs and lungs will be completely overgrown with the fungi.

be tried. This drug however must be administered intravenously, over a period of ten to fourteen days. Treatment is very costly and worthwhile only where valuable birds are involved.

Metabolic Disturbances

VITAMIN-B DEFICIENCY

Incidence: The vitamins of the B-complex are responsible for, among other things, nerve growth and particularly for the conduction of impulses along the nerves. Many of these vitamins can be produced by a bird itself inside the intestine, but the remainder need to be supplied by the food. The vitamins of the B-complex are water-soluble and normally present in the food of parrots in adequate amounts. However, if foods have been frozen for a long time or are simply too old, their vitamin-B content may be considerably reduced. Intestinal disorders and parasitic infestation, notably with *Coccidia*, result in disturbances of vitamin-B balance.

Clinical picture: The disease runs a mild course, at first resulting in general weakness and slight paralysis of the toes and legs. The bird cannot control the legs properly and "hangs" on the perch rather than sits on it. In the advanced stage, refusal of food, diarrhea, and obvious disturbance of the central nervous system are observed. Particularly characteristic is a twisting of the neck and a phenomenon called "star-gazing" [in German]: the bird's head is put well back.

Postmortem: Very inconclusive. Usually the only abnormality that can be seen is muscular atrophy due to restricted movement.

Prevention and treatment: To prevent the condition, the birdkeeper must ensure that his birds are free from parasites and that their diet is as varied as possible. Prolonged freezing of foods should be avoided. Treatment consists of the administration of vitamins of the B-complex in high doses (*e.g.,* Polyvital® , Polybion®), in drop form via the drinking water. Overdoses are not possible. Where the bird's condition was in fact due to vitamin-B deficiency a notable improvement will be seen in one to two days of treatment—unless the bird has already sustained permanent damage to the nervous system.

RICKETS

Synonyms: Osteomalacia, softening of the bones.

Incidence: This metabolic disorder is caused by an inadequate supply of vitamin D in the diet and too low a calcium and phosphorous content. Particularly at risk are young birds that are being hand-reared on the wrong foods.

Clinical picture: To a greater or lesser degree the whole skeleton is involved, although the long bones suffer most. At an advanced stage they can be bent without breaking ("rubber bones"). As a result, the birds are usually unable to perch or stand. They drop their excreta directly under themselves, making the owner at first think of diarrhea-like digestive disorders. In time, all bones show severe curvatures, and false joints and spontaneous fractures occur. As the general health of the patient remains unaffected for a considerable time, only a thorough examination reveals the disease in its early stages.

Diagnosis: Thorough palpation of the skeletal system with some anatomical knowledge as to the position of the joints is often sufficient for the diagnosis. In case of doubt an X-ray will help.

Prevention and treatment: The measures for prevention and treatment are the same: adequate supplies of vitamin D_3 combined with exposure to sunlight for an hour at a time. Where young birds are concerned, a mineral mixture containing plenty of calcium and phosphorus (*e.g.,* Viphoscal ZVT® , Davinova forte®) or simply a powdered calcium supplement should be given. If the disease is very advanced, treatment is no longer successful since the curved bones harden in their unnatural shape when minerals are administered and the bird will no longer be able to survive.

GOUT

Incidence: By gout we understand the depositing of uric acid—normally excreted through the kidney—in the organism. The causes of the condition are not yet fully understood. It may be that food with too high a protein content is responsible or, as has been shown in some cases, that there has been some damage to the organs of excretion, the kidneys. Gout is seen not just in old birds but in all age groups. The most commonly affected species, according to my own observations, is the Budgerigar.

Clinical picture. There are two types of gout: (1) Visceral, or renal, gout runs a rapid course. The only abnormalities shown by the bird are an apathetic behavior and quickly progressing emaciation. Death occurs within a few days after the first morbid signs have become apparent. (2) Gout involving the joints—here the subcutaneous tissue in the region of the joints is seen to contain yellowish white nodules which enclose a substance resembling toothpaste. (These abnormalities are easily mistaken for purulent foci by the inexperienced.) The patient is visibly suffering a lot of pain in the affected joints and refuses to fly or stand on its feet. This form of gout can go on for many weeks before terminating fatally.

Postmortem: In visceral/renal gout, dissection will reveal highly characteristic changes. The kidney looks grayish white and the renal canals appear to the acute eye as elongated, white needles. The remaining organs—notably pericardium, liver, and air sacs—look as though dusted with powdered sugar. All these changes are due to deposits of uric acid. Where the joints are involved, all affected joints are filled with a whitish creamy substance.

Diagnosis: In cases of visceral gout a diagnosis is not possible while the patient is alive, although the passing of watery urine may sometimes hint at the condition.

Prevention and treatment: If gout is suspected, the protein content of the diet should be reduced drastically. The additional administration of vitamin A in high doses is recommended. There is no known cure.

Other Abnormalities

AXILLARY DERMATITIS IN BUDGERIGARS AND LOVEBIRDS

Cause: Various bacteria and fungi, perhaps also viruses in combination with stressful situations.

Incidence: Budgerigars and lovebirds (also one case, in my own practice, of a Cockatiel) are affected by a disease which confines itself to certain areas of the skin. The cause of this disease is as yet not fully understood.

Clinical picture: Usually on the underside of the wing, in the axilla, the patients show a skin change which resembles a tear. The area concerned tends to be crusty and matted with blood. The surrounding tissue is yellowish, with a raised swelling. Presumably because of itchiness, these skin areas are persistently pecked at by the bird, and the blood on the bird's beak eventually draws the owner's attention to the condition. Because of flying activity, the affected area usually cannot heal; if it does heal, it is immediately torn open again. Usually these symptoms occur unilaterally, more rarely bilaterally or on other areas of the body. One notable fact is that this skin disease occurs suddenly in birds which have been perfectly healthy for years but recently suffered considerable stress (*e.g.,* due to unsuccessful breeding or territorial squabbles). Left untreated, the birds often die after weeks of illness.

Possible treatment: Broad-spectrum antibiotics in combination with antimycotics in ointment form applied several times a day over a period of about eight days can effect a cure (*e.g.,* Terracortil® ointment and Moronal® ointment applied alternately.) It must be pointed out, however, that a large percentage of birds will suffer a relapse in the same or a different area of the skin. An operation whereby the affected tissue is removed in its entirety is promising, too. After the operation a bandage must be applied and the wing involved immobilized.

FEATHER PLUCKING

Incidence: Feather plucking occurs in a great many parrots including the larger species and cockatoos. Affected birds tend to be those who are kept by themselves, as family pets. Breeding birds may, however, also become pluckers, although they do not mutilate themselves but pluck out the growing feathers of their young.

Clinical picture: For reasons that remain a mystery to the owner, affected birds start to peck at their own plumage. In the early stages they usually attack the small feathers on the shoulders and breast. At a later stage, however, the large feathers are not spared

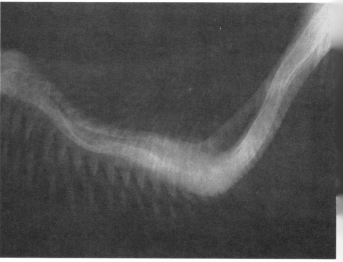

A Budgerigar with severe disturbance of the central nervous system due to vitamin-B deficiency. Despite the involuntary twisting of the head, birds in this state are usually still able to eat.

X-ray of the wing of a bird suffering from rickets (softening of the bones). Particularly conspicuous is the wave-like bending of the humerus, radius, and ulna.

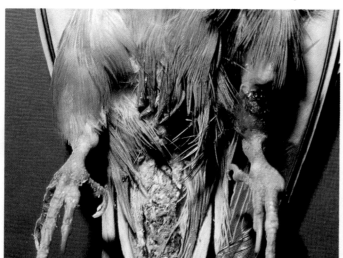

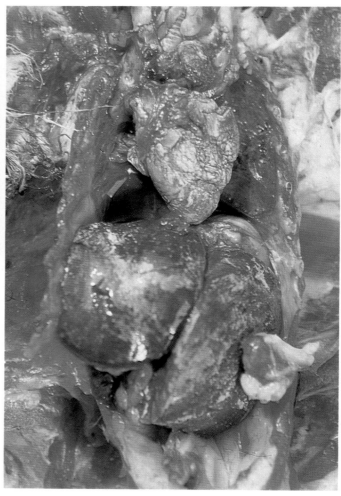

Above: Gout nodules on the feet of a Budgerigar. In addition, the severly pasted vent may be seen. This pasting with salts of uric acid is common in renal diseases. It is not due to diarrhea but is the result of changes in the consistency of the normally creamy urine.

Right: Section of a parrot with visceral gout. The whitish deposits of uric acid on the liver (center) and the heart (top) are clearly visible.

Budgerigar with a tumor behind the eye. The pressure of the growing tumor forces the eye outwards.

Typical site of the skin change in a Budgerigar with axillary dermatitis.

A large tumor in the abdominal cavity of a Budgerigar.

Tumor of the testes of a Budgerigar. Note the changed color of the cere of this male bird. The sex-specific blue color has changed to the brown of a female because the tumor has prevented production of male sex hormones.

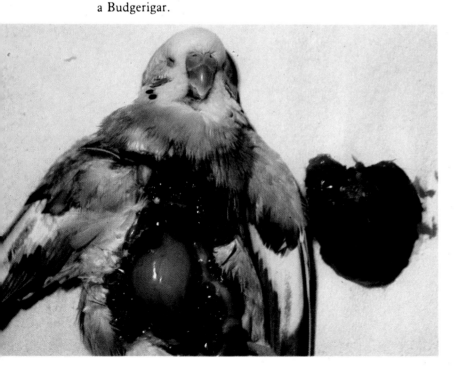

either, which ultimately results in complete nakedness (apart from the head which, of course, the bird cannot reach with its beak). Often the bird does not stop at its feathers but attacks its own skin and even the musculature.

Causes: Although the exact cause of feather plucking is not known, emotional disturbance is the basis for this abnormal behavior. The loss of the human being upon whom a bird has been imprinted is a possible cause, as boredom may be. In parrot-imprinted (wild-caught) birds, constant stress—can be the precipitating factor. In some cases the onset of sexual maturity has been identified as a possible cause—the bird lacked a partner with which it could engage in instinctive modes of behavior.

Possible treatment: It is necessary in every case to establish the possible cause so that this can be eliminated. First one needs to find out whether the patient is man- or parrot-imprinted, as this is important when it comes to treatment. Wherever possible one should try keeping the parrot outdoors, *e.g.,*, in the garden on a tree, if possible. Acquiring a second bird of the same species may also prove helpful—with the disadvantage, however, that the birds will no longer be as tame as one might wish. The application of sprays or other preparations has no effect whatsoever on feather plucking.

TUMORS

Incidence: Tumors occur in all parrots but are particularly common in Budgerigars. Budgerigars in the four to six-year age group appear to be especially susceptible. The disease is of little significance in aviary birds but very common in Budgerigars kept in cages.

Clinical picture: Birds suffering from tumors are of poor general health with severe weight loss despite a good food intake. In the case of large tumors in the abdominal cavity, dyspnea is an additional sign since the viscera exert pressure on the lungs and air sacs. Particularly in cases of tumors in the region of the reproductive organs and the kidneys, unilateral paralysis of the legs may be observed (resulting from pressure on the nerve which supplies the limb concerned). Where a bird suffers from tumors under the skin—usually benign adipose tumors—growths up to walnut-size can be felt; these tumors do no usually affect the general health.

Postmortem: Depending on types and site of the tumors, pinhead to walnut-sized greasy coarse, lumpy enlargements of the involved organs are observed. Female birds frequently suffer from tumors of the ovaries, male bird from tumors of the testes. Whether a growth i benign or malignant cannot be determined without cytological examination.

Diagnosis: Tumors must be suspected where the following factors apply: (1) Four to six year age group (exceptionally, however, young or older birds may be affected). (2) Weight loss despite a good food intake. (3) The bird sleep the whole day and only wakes up to feed. (4 In the case of renal tumors: unilateral paralysi of a leg (where sprains, fractures, or othe mechanical injuries can be excluded). An x-ray may help to confirm the diagnosis.

Prevention and treatment: Prevention is no possible since the causes of tumors are no known. The only treatment that can be con sidered is surgical intervention. How suc cessful an operation is likely to be depends on the stage of development and site of the tumor. In the case of tumors originating from the ovary or oviduct the chances of a suc cessful outcome are not unfavorable.

Bibliography

Alderton, David. 1979. *Lovebirds: Their Care and Breeding.* K & R Books, Edlington, Lincolnshire.

Arnall, L., and Keymer, I.F. 1975. *Bird Diseases.* T.F.H. Publications, Neptune, N.J.

Aschenborn, Carl. 1978. *Die Papageien.* Albrecht Philler Verlag, Minden.

Bedford, Duke of. 1969. *Parrots and Parrot-like Birds.* T.F.H. Publications, Neptune, N.J.

Biggs, John. 1981. *Lovebirds: Answers to Your Questions.* J-P Publishers, San Bernardino, Calif.

Boetticher, Hans von. 1959. *Papageien.* Ziemsen-Verlag, Wittenberg.

Burr, Elisha. 1982. *Diseases of Parrots.* T.F.H. Publications, Neptune, N.J.

Dost, Helmut. 1973. *Sittiche und Papageien.* VOB Buch u. Offsetdruck, Leipzig.

Enehjelm, Curt af. 1979. *Papageien.* Franckh'sche Verlagshandlung, Stuttgart.

Fischer, Rudolf. 1978. *Papageien und Sittiche.* M. & H. Schaper, Hannover.

Forshaw, Joseph M. 1977. *Parrots of the World.* T.F.H. Publications, Neptune, N.J.

Grahl, Wolfgang de. 1972. *Papageien in Haus und Garten.* Ulmer-Verlag, Stuttgart
———. 1974. *Papageien unserer Erde.* Wolfgang de Grahl, Hamburg.

Hampe, Helmut. 1957. *Die Unzertrennlichen.* Gottfried Helene, Pfungstadt.

Hayward, Jim. 1979. *Lovebirds and Their Color Mutations.* Blandford Press, Poole, Dorset.

Lichtenstadt, S. 1898. *Zwerg- und Zierpapageien.* Modes Verlag, Berlin.

Low, Rosemary. 1980. *Parrots: Their Care and Breeding.* Blandford Press, Poole, Dorset.

Neunzig, Karl. 1921. *Fremdländische Stubenvögel.* Creutz'sche Verlagshandlung, Magdeburg.

Pinter, Helmut. 1979. *Handbuch der Papageienkunde.* Franckh'sche Verlagshandlung. Stuttgart.

Plath, Karl, and Davis Malcolm. 1971. *This is the Parrot.* T.F.H. Publications, Neptune, N.J.

Radtke, Georg A. 1981. *The T.F.H. Book of Lovebirds.* T.F.H. Publications, Neptune, N.J.

Raethel, Heinz-Sigurd. 1981. *Bird Diseases.* T.F.H. Publications, Neptune, N.J.

Reichenow, A. 1955. *Papageien.* Gottfried Helene, Pfungstadt.

Russ, Karl. 1898. *Die sprechenden Papageien.* Creutz'sche Verlagshandlung, Magdeburg.
———. 1881. *Die Papageien.* Creutz'sche Verlagshandlung, Magdeburg.

Rutgers, A., and Norris, K.A. (eds.) 1972. *Encyclopaedia of Aviculture.* Blandford Press, Poole, Dorset.

Schwichtenberg, Heinz. 1973. *Die Unzertrennlichen.* Ziemsen-Verlag, Wittenberg.

Silva, Tony, and Kotlar, Barbara. 1981. *Breeding Lovebirds.* T.F.H. Publications, Neptune, N.J.

Smith, George A. 1979. *Lovebirds and Related Parrots.* T.F.H. Publications, Neptune, N.J.

Teitler, Risa. 1979. *Taming and Training Lovebirds.* T.F.H. Publications, Neptune, N.J.

Vriends, Matthew M. 1978. *Encyclopedia of Lovebirds and other Dwarf Parrots.* T.F.H. Publications, Neptune, N.J.

Walraven, Chr. 1974. *Onze Papegaai.* De Regenboog, Amsterdam.

Agapornis World, monthly journal of The African Lovebird Society (Box 142, San Marcos, CA 92069).

The Avicultural Magazine, journal of The Avicultural Society (Windsor Forest Stud, Mill Ride, Ascot, Berkshire SL5 8LT, England).

AZ-Nachrichten (AZN), monthly journal of the Austauschzentrale der Vogelliebhaber und -Zuchter Deutschlands (Vor der Elm 1, 286 Osterholz-Scharmbeck, Germany).

Die Gefiederte Welt, monthly journal (VFV Verbands- und Fachschriftenverlag GmbH & Co., Wiesbadener Str. 63, 6503 Mainz-Kastel, Germany).

A pair of Dutch Blue Peach-faced
Lovebirds (photo by H. Reinhard).

Index

Page numbers in boldface refer to illustrations.

HANDBOOK OF LOVEBIRDS
HORST BIELFELD